A
Cup
of
Comfort
for Parents of
Children with Autism

Stories of Hope and Everyday Success

 EDITED BY
COLLEEN SELL

FOREWORD BY
DOUG AND LAURIE FLUTIE
FOUNDERS OF THE DOUG FL...
FOUNDATION FOR A...

ADAMS...
Avon, Massa...

In memory of our beloved Buddy.

Published by
Adams Media, an F+W Publications Company
57 Littlefield Street, Avon, MA 02322 U.S.A.
www.adamsmedia.com and *www.cupofcomfort.com*

ISBN 10: 1-59337-683-9
ISBN 13: 978-1-59337-683-3

Printed in the United States of America.

J I H G F E D C B

Library of Congress Cataloging-in-Publication Data
available from the publisher.

This publication is designed to provide accurate and authoritative information
with regard to the subject matter covered. It is sold with the understanding that
the publisher is not engaged in rendering legal, accounting, or other professional
advice. If legal advice or other expert assistance is required, the services of a
competent professional person should be sought.
    —From a *Declaration of Principles* jointly adopted by a Committee of the
American Bar Association and a Committee of Publishers and Associations

Many of the designations used by manufacturers and sellers to distinguish
their products are claimed as trademarks. Where those designations appear in
this book and Adams Media was aware of a trademark claim, the designations
have been printed with initial capital letters.

*This book is available at quantity discounts for bulk purchases.
For information, please call 1-800-289-0963.*

 Acknowledgments

I would first like to acknowledge the millions of children and adults with autism and their loved ones for their courage and compassion and for all the good they bring to the world.

My sincere appreciation goes to the authors whose terrific stories grace these pages.

As always, the terrific team at Adams Media has gone above and beyond in making this a rewarding experience and producing an excellent book. I am especially thankful to Laura Daly for jumping in to steer the Cup of Comfort ship and to the captains of the ship, Paula Munier and Gary Krebs.

I would be remiss were I not to acknowledge my husband, family, and dear friends for supporting me in my work and for dragging me away from my desk to enjoy them once in a while.

 Contents

Foreword

When our son Dougie was diagnosed with autism at age three, we asked the same question as other parents in our situation: "What do you mean, autism? We can't have a child who has a problem." But we quickly learned not to dwell on the diagnosis—and to instead focus on our amazing son.

True, caring for Dougie is a twenty-four-hour job. But all it takes is one flash of his brilliant smile to wipe away any weariness we may sometimes feel. We experience all kinds of special moments with Dougie, who loves to swim and listen to music in the car. One summer afternoon, on our way to his water-sports camp, we told Dougie where we were going and his whole face lit up with excitement. He also gets very excited when he knows we are on our way to his therapeutic horseback riding lesson. It is these moments of understanding and excitement that we appreciate and wouldn't trade for anything.

In the following pages, you'll read dozens of moving stories about families just like ours—families that face the challenges with courage and welcome the triumphs with joy.

All over the world, children with autism are growing up and realizing their full potential, thanks to the love and support of their families, who understand their kids' needs better than anyone. These children are now being given better opportunities than they ever have before. They are attending regular schools, making friends, and developing into well-rounded, happy individuals. Clearly, this is progress, but we—parents, loved ones, and our community—can do more.

Knowing firsthand how much time, effort, and money goes into caring for a child with autism, we've established the Doug Flutie, Jr. Foundation for Autism (*www.dougflutiejrfoundation.org*). The Foundation's mission is threefold: 1) to aid financially disadvantaged families who need assistance in caring for their children with autism; 2) to fund education and research into the causes and consequences of childhood autism; and 3) to serve as a clearinghouse and communications center for new programs and services developed for individuals with autism.

This Foundation is our legacy to Dougie. It's our way to give back to the children, parents, teachers, and caregivers who've helped us do the best by our son.

All our children deserve the best of our love and support—because they unfailingly give us their best, no matter what. Each of the inspiring stories found within the pages of this book serves as a reminder of this. We hope you'll enjoy A *Cup of Comfort for Parents of Children with Autism*, and celebrate, along with us, the myriad ways our kids enrich and enliven our lives.

Because every child is a blessing.

—*Doug and Laurie Flutie*

# Introduction

> *"Being deeply loved gives you strength,*
> *loving deeply gives you courage."*
> Lao Tso

During the many months I worked on this book, I was asked repeatedly the same two questions by people living within the world of autism: "Do you have a loved one on the autism spectrum?" and "Why a book of personal stories about autism?"

The short answers are: There is no autism among my inner circle of family and friends . . . yet. The main reason the publisher, Adams Media, and I wanted to do this book is because we care deeply about children with autism and their families and believe their stories need to be told.

It has been said that you cannot fully understand something until you've experienced it. As the mother of two grown children who are not "neuro-typical" (though neither of them falls into the "special needs" category), I came to understand what I'd once only imagined—what it's like to be the parent of a unique child who has challenges that are often invisible to the casual observer. So I know how my children's love for me gave me strength and how my love for them gave me the courage and wherewithal to help them move beyond their disorders. And I understand the value of connecting with other parents of children with different needs.

Certainly, the same is true of parents of children with autism—a large and growing group of people from all walks of life. According to the Centers for Disease Control, the rate of autism has increased significantly over the past twenty years, from 1 in 2,000 American children in the mid-1980s to 1 in 160 in 2004. This trend is mirrored in other industrialized countries, most notably Canada and the United Kingdom. Despite the progress that has been made in diagnosing, understanding, and treating autism, there is still no cure, and there is still a lack of understanding and resources. Though these deficits cannot be remedied with this or any book, I believe strongly in the power of story to comfort and inspire, to heal and to help, and to connect us with one another.

That is exactly the power within each of the essays in A Cup of Comfort for Parents of Children with

Autism. I hope these heartwarming true stories—written by ordinary people about their extraordinary children—will bring you comfort and hope.

Colleen Sell

Part of the Gift

My wife and I sit together on one of the couches in the doctor's examining room, which is at least 30 feet long with many toys in plastic bins.

"Yep, he's autistic," the doctor says nonchalantly, labeling our son as if she were stating the color of his hair.

Looking over at my little boy as he plays with a figurine of a knight on a galloping horse, I find her diagnosis impossible to believe. He's too engaged in the world around him. Because I work with disabled children at a mental health hospital, the doctor had asked me if I thought Sawyer had autism. I had said no. He is too loving and too involved with me and his mom and two sisters. No, he didn't respond much to the doctor, but he is only three.

Yet, afterward as we eat lunch and even though Sawyer is strangely well behaved, the diagnosis also makes sense in many ways. He does have some sensory issues; he is evasive and shy around grandparents and strangers; and he does not talk yet. The diagnosis crushes the shield of denial that has obscured my vision, and I begin to grieve the loss of my son's future. It is suddenly set in stone that Sawyer's life will become three years of in-home therapy followed by special education classrooms and Individualized Education Plan team meetings. I'm a special education teacher in a place where the children live behind locked doors because they have severe disabilities and have failed everyplace else. So I'm jaded and can only perceive that autism means Sawyer will not experience normal friendships, cub scouts, sports, girlfriends.

Later at a conference on in-home therapy, a presenter states that only ten percent of people with autism lead independent lives. I leave the conference with those terrifying words echoing in my mind— confirmation that Sawyer will miss out on a career, falling in love, and having kids of his own.

Everything becomes a race against time. In Wisconsin, children with autism receive Medicaid funding for three years of in-home therapy. I want the most out of it. My wife looks forward to the lifting of the financial burden of diapers when funding for them starts at age four. I look at his being in diapers at age four as a defeat. There is a theory that children have something called a language acquisition device (LAD), a process where they gain speech at a faster rate than adults. I worry that Sawyer will miss some magical window to use LAD to master language. Really, I want to reach the goal of "normal by kindergarten."

"Sawyer, come use your potty chair." I prop Sawyer's Buddy doll on the potty chair. This stuffed guy with his baby face and red coveralls is ignored by Sawyer and slated for Goodwill, but I think I can put him to use. "Sawyer, come use your potty chair. See, Buddy's a big boy."

Sawyer laughs to see his doll on the potty. I want to show Sawyer that the potty chair is perfectly harmless and fun. But he won't sit on the chair without crying. Exhausted from teaching all day, I go back to work with him on the flashcards that the early childhood instructor had sent as homework. I use my teaching techniques to push Sawyer toward progress. I give M&Ms paired with verbal praise as rewards, but I am, frankly, frustrated. Then Sawyer gets up and carries Buddy into the bathroom.

Sure enough, Buddy has to pee-pee. Sawyer resists even sitting on the potty, but Buddy starts going on a fairly regular basis. With Sawyer's prompting, Buddy tinkles as I pour water between his fiber-stuffed legs. Night after night, Buddy does everything Sawyer does . . . or rather, does it for him. Buddy goes in the high chair to eat and signs for "all done." Sawyer defers the flashcards to Buddy. I have Buddy pick the right card and reward him with a "good job!" and an M&M. Sawyer loves that and wants Buddy to keep going. Sawyer even occasionally takes a turn, and Buddy is a big help as he gives high fives and hugs when Sawyer picks the right card, but I begin to wonder if Buddy has as much chance of talking as Sawyer.

Then one night Sawyer gets down off my lap and places Buddy on my lap as a stand-in for him. This is a spark of imaginative play I've hoped he would develop. But although I think it's sweet that Sawyer is concerned I might get lonely, I am a little upset that he is not learning from his little role model. I don't want the pretend boy. I want my boy. But I also dream of Sawyer not having autism.

My wife and I sit in the little early childhood class chairs at the first IEP meeting I attend, where I feel like I am being judged on how good a parent I am. It's not what anyone says or does; it's just how I feel. Sawyer's teacher, speech therapist, and occupational therapist all report good things.

"He's doing well," his teacher says. "He is learning the picture exchange program (PEC) quite well. So well, in fact, that when I was teaching Sawyer how to use a PEC of an apple to get an apple, he went over to someone else's desk and stole the PEC for a cookie."

We all laugh, because Sawyer is smart and a scoundrel at times, but part of me frets because he has to learn a nonverbal form of communication.

Sawyer's life becomes twenty-five hours of therapy and twelve hours of early childhood education a week. This, for a boy whose whole world had been his parents and two older sisters. He balks sometimes, refusing to put on his shoes because it means riding the bus to school. The arrival of a therapist often makes Sawyer come over and swat the nearest parent and have a small tantrum.

I feel for him, but I feel the pressure of time more. I know that we have to press forward. I want to push past the situations that prevent Sawyer from normalcy and that squeeze my heart like a peeled banana in a baby's grasp. Sawyer wants so badly to be friends with kids he sees on playgrounds. But without language, he simply goes up to kids and growls at them like Simba in *The Lion King*, which doesn't make him too popular. Without language, getting his desires across is difficult.

I push Sawyer on our old metal swing set as I sit in front of him. I really want to stop, but because at one time, he didn't like swinging, I renew the pushes as he makes the sign for more. With every push, I want to believe that the sensation will make his autism better. Lessen the affliction. But this small task, the simple act of giving a loved one all that he wants for the moment, is powerful. These moments, with his laughter and my hands on his knees pushing him as we feel the warmth of the sun behind western clouds, are so good that it makes me believe that the future will be good.

Megan, Sawyer's therapist, asks him to point to the picture that begins with the S sound. Instead, Sawyer jumps up and points to the porch. He is not talking yet, but does things that impress us. When it rains, he stands at the window and twinkles his fingers—the sign for rain. His response to pointing to the picture that begins with P is to sprint to his bedroom to bring back a puzzle. But it looks like Sawyer is off-base with the letter S. That is, until one of the therapists realizes that weeks ago he saw a spider on the porch. The therapists handle the flashcards now, giving my family their evenings back. The evenings are even better because Sawyer's spirit catches on fire by impressing the new women (the therapists) in his life. That fire ignites my soul, like using a birthday candle to light the rest.

Now that he is talking in two-word sentences, he often recites who is home: "Mama, Papa, Mo (Morgan), Tristen (Kristen)." He will repeat our names several times and seems to take joy in knowing who is with him, as we take joy in being his safe zone. He also runs around the house repeating, "Ciao bella," which is Italian for "Hello, beautiful." This is the other thing that taught me to take one day at a time: my son's love of silliness, learning, and his family. If silliness, learning, and his family are enough for Sawyer, why can't it be enough for all of us? My worry of the future has turned to savoring the slow progress.

He is our last child, and without worrying about the future, I am in no hurry for him to catch up as long as he is happy. And he is happy. At four, he is going through his terrible twos phase and is enjoying his newfound power of being oppositional. He likes to respond to requests with "No way" or even "I'm fine."

"Sawyer, time for bed."

"No way. I'm fine."

There will always be new worries. He does have some pronoun confusion, for example, saying "chase you" when he means "chase me." He gets upset when things are not as he thinks they should be. When his ever-lounging teenage sister occasionally ventures out of her room, Sawyer demands, "Tristen, upastairs!" But then, I don't know what to make of her being downstairs with her boring family either.

If Sawyer were not talking and not making progress, I do not know if I could believe the future would be as good. We are the lucky ones. I cannot feel self-pity for long, even though we are in year five of changing diapers, in part because I know that my son has lesser challenges than many other children out there. It also comes from the realization that my son is not a child with an affliction but a child with autism. And it is only part of who he is, just like a child might have blond hair, small feet, or a talent for singing. In other words, autism is part of the gift, not the part of the gift that got damaged.

Just days ago, Sawyer's school had early dismissal, and he had his therapy session before, rather than after, I got home from work. I had missed my usual treasured time alone with him, from the time he gets off the school bus until his therapy starts. So when I walked in our house, I immediately scooped him up and squeezed him. That was when Sawyer described the gift he has given his parents. As his therapist rounded the corner, she asked Sawyer, "What is Daddy doing?"

"Loving," he said.

Thomas Cannon

Blazing New Trails

It is one of those gorgeous Indian summer days that makes going for a run feel like I am getting away with something. I love this time of year, when late summer warmth combines with early fall colors. Everything is especially inviting, because it really should be the beginning of the cold, slippery winter. And on this early Saturday morning, I have time to run without the jog stroller—time alone to think and time to not think at all. I don't know why, but the sound of my shoes hitting the trail gives me the tiny hope that I can make sense out of life. Of course, I never know how the things I haven't been dealing with while standing still are going to resurface midstride.

As I reach the bike path, I start out with an easy jog and my thoughts wander. Let's see. Laundry is in progress. Got groceries yesterday morning. When I get home I'll have time to vacuum and dust before starting dinner for our friends Dave and Mark, who are coming over tonight. Two-year-old Terry has been fed and dressed and was playing with his favorite puzzles when I left. All seems in order.

Stretching my legs and letting my mind run free for the first time in too long feels good. All I have to think about is my feet hitting the trail. The thump, thump, thump of my own footsteps is all I hear.

Once I'm warmed up, I pick up the pace a bit. Just enjoy the run. No need to focus on the waiting, the worrying. Look at the leaves in that park ahead—incredible.

Slowly, the fear sneaks in, sifting through the autumn foliage. A *Parents* magazine article I read this week returns to my consciousness: a father's story about his eight-year-old son who has autism, still throwing tantrums and still in diapers. I knew I shouldn't have let myself read it. Ever determined to read the magazines I subscribe to, I had picked up this old issue from last January. I should have skipped right over to the "Best and Worst Cold Remedies for Kids," which was the reason I'd chosen this issue to read instead of last February's or even the newly arrived October issue. There'd been no warning on the cover to protect me from the power this article would wield in my mind. As I flipped toward the cold remedies piece, the title, "What It's Really Like to Raise a Child with Autism," grabbed hold of me. I should have fought my way free.

The father sounded tired, though his love for his son was obvious, even inspiring. His patience seemed endless. His son, now strong-willed and too big to carry, is unable to communicate his needs, unable to care much for himself. What would it be like to have a child for eight years and never have a real conversation, to play that guessing game, the trial and error of solving every unhappiness, every little problem?

My legs suddenly stop running. I step off the trail to catch my breath and pull myself together. This never happens. I feel like, in this relay, instead of a baton, someone has passed me an anvil. I lean against a tree and pretend to stretch a tight calf muscle as an older couple walks past me. Shake it off, shake it off. This isn't helpful. Breathe. Think clearly. Just get moving again.

What if Terry never says more than the few words he has known for almost a year? We made a conscious decision not to worry until he turned two. We took heart in the pediatrician's lack of concern. We tried to ignore the mounting evidence. Then, we celebrated his second birthday.

I walk for a few minutes, glad to have sunglasses to cover the chilling tears sliding down my sweaty face. I don't know how to be a good mom. I don't know if I can do what that father does. What if I am not strong enough? It is going to be so hard to figure out. I don't know what to do. I probably shouldn't be out on this run. So selfish of me. I should be doing . . . something. I'm not sure what, but . . . something.

Walk turns to jog, and jog turns to run. Slow run. This barely meets the definition of running. Consciously move each foot forward. Swing my arms. Breathe. Let go brain, let go. I need to feel the trail beneath me and the warm sunshine bathing my skin again. Focus on the clump of aspen trees ahead. We should head up into the high country to check it all out. Maybe a weekend away would help us all. Thump, thump, thump.

So many indications, so many red flags had gone unnoticed. Terry is more independent than other toddlers. He can spin anything, from a puzzle piece to his dad's wedding ring. He is a rigidly picky eater who won't touch finger foods. He is the only child we know who screams at the park when I put sunscreen on him or who likes to watch the world through my translucent red toothbrush. The more we read, the more we realize that what we considered simple personality quirks, talents, and slight delays are line-item symptoms of ASD, autism spectrum disorder. Now we are sure, though we are still waiting for the official diagnosis.

Carefully, I focus on each breath of warm fall air. Slow run, but at least I am still moving. Smells of dried leaves and crushed crabapples start to distract me from the weight I am carrying. Come on, Christy, get it together. I can make sense out of this somehow. Life with Terry is amazing, wonderful, happy. I love him with all my heart. I have done lots of hard things before. I know how to work hard. How many tough, at-risk kids have I taught how to read, to multiply, to feel safe at school? How did I survive the lonely feeling of living in another country by myself, understanding so little of what was said around me? I know how to commit to something important. Maybe hard work won't fix it, but I will work my hardest to figure it out. I will do anything, absolutely anything, to be the best mom I can be for my son.

Then it hits me like a wave of cool air: I don't have to take care of that boy in the magazine. I stop, astonished at this realization.

The tears feel warmer now. Everything feels lighter. Back to running again, faster now. Just because we are figuring out that Terry, the two-year-old love of our lives, also has autism doesn't mean everything is suddenly changing. We don't have to trade him in for that magazine kid when we get the final diagnosis. When we hear that official report, we won't love or enjoy him a single ounce less. So maybe our parent job descriptions are changing, and maybe we'll spend our days differently than what we had envisioned. He will always be our Terry, our sweet little boy. We will always be a family. The effect of this good news is exhilarating. I sprint the last mile home.

I don't know how to take care of an eight-year-old with autism. Someday, maybe I will. But it will be my eight-year-old, my Terry, and I will have six more joy-filled years of experience by then. Who knows, maybe we will write our own article someday.

I round the corner and slow my pace as I head up the walkway to our house. Through the window I see them: father and son in the middle of a tickle war.

"Looks like you two are having a great time this morning," I say, stretching my hamstrings and catching my breath.

"Yep. Terry, who's that? Who's that?"

With Marv's help, Terry looks up toward me in the doorway. "Mama!"

I sweep him up into my arms just as he arrives from his sprint across the room, and I realize I wouldn't change a thing about my life. None of us knows what lies ahead on this journey with autism. It is a different trail than the one we set out for. But now I realize that through all the twists and turns, we will run it together.

Christy Shoemaker

 Searching for Normal

I always knew that some day I would be a mother. As a child, baby dolls were my favorite toys. I loved dressing them, feeding them, holding their small bodies in my arms and swaying back and forth. I learned how to diaper, dress, and feed a baby from those plastic-bodied beings.

What I hadn't learned during those hours of make-believe was how to cope with the emotional needs of a child. Nor how to comfort an infant who cries for hours. Nor how to calm a toddler who throws herself down in the middle of a grocery store in a fit of rage. Nor how to deal with my emotions when the child I gave birth to didn't behave the way I'd dreamed she would.

My daughter, Emily, taught me those things.

My mother is visiting from Michigan. Emily is four years old. Emily is being defiant and not putting away her toys as I've asked. I'm trying to get Emily to sit quietly for four minutes, the time-out method of discipline espoused in all the parenting books I read so diligently. The books make it sound easy. They don't know Emily. She refuses to sit, refuses to be quiet, refuses to do the simple thing I have asked her to do. Eventually, she begins crying hysterically and yelling.

"I'm going to set the timer," I tell her in the calmest voice I can manage. "For every minute that you keep yelling, you are going to have a minute added to your time out." This is another tactic of the parenting experts.

"No, Mom," she screams. "Don't set the timer."

She runs from the dining room into the kitchen to stop me. I punch numbers into the timer on the microwave. With each beep, the pitch of her voice rises.

"I said no!" she yells. "I'll stop, I promise."

I pause, my finger hovering over the timer as I watch for signs that she is calming down. But she doesn't stop yelling. She only keeps yelling that she will stop. I finish setting the timer and take her hand to lead her back into the dining room. She jerks away from me. My voice starts to rise.

"If you don't go back into that chair right now," I threaten, "I am going to take away your toys." The books say to take away one toy at a time until the child behaves. But I am beyond the reasoning found in these books.

"Noooo!" she wails. She is now so distraught that she falls to the floor.

I start the countdown. "Ten . . ."

"Stop counting," she yells.

"Nine . . ."

"Please, Mom," still sitting on the floor.

"Eight . . ."

"I said I would stop." The anger rises in her voice.

"Seven . . ."

"I said to stop counting." She is no longer pleading, but demanding.

"Six . . ."

She can only scream.

"Five. . . . Are you going to calm down?

My question sparks a new surge of anger.

"Four . . ."

More screaming.

"Three . . ."

"Don't you do it, Mom!"

"Two. . . . This is your last chance."

"Mooooom!"

"One."

I turn my back to her and storm up the stairs to her room. She follows me, still screaming. The countdown has not calmed either one of us.

Methodically, I start to remove things from her room. Her stuffed animals. Her doll house. Her LEGOs. Finally, her room is bare. She has slumped into a puddle on the floor. I close the door on her and go to my room. My mother has taken refuge there. I sit beside her as I cry.

"I don't know what to do with her," I say.

"Well, I know what I would do," my mother replies. "It seems to me like she needs a good spanking."

"Spanking doesn't work either," I confess. "It only makes her angrier."

The one time I resorted to spanking, too frustrated to know what else to do, Emily looked at me with shocked indignation.

"You hit me," she said, eyes wide, hands on her hips. "Why did you hit me?"

"Because I want you to listen to me," I replied.

"But you hit me. You said no hitting."

My mother doesn't understand this. "I know one thing," she says. "You kids never talked to me and your dad the way she talks to you."

"I know," I say. She is right. We never did. Growing up, it never would have crossed my mind to behave the way my daughter does.

I am too exhausted to talk about it anymore. I can only sit and wonder where I went wrong, why this child is so defiant and difficult. My mother sits beside me. I wonder whether she is asking herself the same thing, wondering where she went wrong, questioning how she failed to teach me to be a good mother.

It doesn't occur to me that Emily might have a disability. It will be nine more years before I understand this, before the terms Asperger's syndrome and autism spectrum disorder become a part of my vocabulary. All I know until then is that her behavior is not "normal," at least not by the definition of normal I have come to believe.

Emily makes her way through toddlerhood remaining isolated from her peers. She enters kindergarten having taught herself to read, although it takes her teacher half the year to realize this.

In first grade, we begin the first of many consultations with educators about Emily's behavior. Her teacher suggests Emily has a learning disability. Subsequent evaluations reveal she is "gifted." In the meeting we have with the professionals from her school, the enhanced learning program (ELP) teacher tells us, "This behavior is normal for a child with Emily's intelligence." It is the first time anyone has used the word normal to define Emily.

Emily enters the ELP program at her school. She is being challenged intellectually, but she still has no friends. Although I am happy for her gifts, there are times when I see her intelligence as one more thing that distances her from the people around her. There are times when I would trade every ninety-ninth percentile ranking on a standardized test for one invitation to a birthday party or for one day when she comes home from school bubbling with the exciting news that her best friend is getting a new puppy and has invited her over to see it after dinner. I would be willing to sacrifice her high intelligence for social acceptability.

When I examine that still dark place inside me, I realize that this wish is not just so that she will be happier but also so that I can be relieved of some of my guilt. More than I want her to be a genius or to succeed academically, I want people to like her. I want people to feel comfortable around her and to acknowledge that I have done my job as a mother to prepare her for the socialized world in which we live. I want this for her, but I also want it for myself. I need to know that I have not failed at the one thing I have always known I wanted to do.

Emily's challenges in the classroom continue into third grade. The concerns of her teacher prompt more evaluations, evaluations resulting in a diagnosis of attention deficit/hyperactivity disorder (ADHD). I think we have found a more appropriate answer to her personality. But medications that typically help children with ADHD only serve to agitate Emily.

When we finally decide to stop the meds after nearly eight months, Emily says "Thanks, Mom. They always gave me such a stomachache."

It pains me to realize she has suffered in silence. I choose to ignore the ADHD diagnosis, telling myself that Emily is simply "quirky"—that it is my idea of parenthood that is flawed.

Emily starts the sixth grade in September 2002. She attends a large public middle school in suburban Minneapolis. I am terrified.

I haven't yet learned that there is a name for Emily's idiosyncrasies. I haven't yet discovered that there are professionals who can help. I don't yet know these things. But I soon will.

Shortly after spring break, I drive to pick up Emily from school. She comes to the van without her backpack. She tells me her teachers would like to talk to me. Emily waits in the media center as I meet with her teachers in a conference room.

"We told Emily we wanted to talk to you about makeup work from when you were on vacation," her history teacher begins. "But that's not really why we asked you here. We have some concerns about Emily."

"Oh?" I say. "What kinds of concerns?" As if I don't know what he will say. As if I haven't been in this conversation with every teacher she has ever had.

"Have you ever considered that there might be a touch of autism in Emily's personality?" her homeroom teacher asks.

This is not what I expected. I have never heard this word associated with my daughter. I am defensive, using denial to protect myself from this assault.

"What makes you think something like that?" I ask.

The history teacher interrupts, "It's not really for us to say. We are just wondering if you would consider talking to the school psychologist about this."

I tell them I will have to think about it and leave the meeting.

Driving home I become angry with these teachers for suggesting such a thing. It is not so much that I disagree, but I am not ready for this label to be applied to my child.

Later, when Emily is in bed and the house is quiet, I look up autism on the Internet. A Google search leads me to the Autism Society of America Web site, where the term Asperger's syndrome is listed. As I read about Asperger's, I feel as though someone has met Emily and is describing her to me. Everything fits. Her behaviors are all normal for someone afflicted with this condition. For the first time in twelve years, I think I might truly understand my child. For the first time in twelve years, I feel her challenges might not be my fault.

The next day I make an appointment to talk with the school psychologist.

It will take several months to receive a formal diagnosis for Emily, and another year to find a psychologist specializing in Asperger's syndrome who is willing to take Emily as a new client. But, within months of receiving treatment, a shift occurs in Emily and in me. Emily starts to make friends. She looks people in the eye when she speaks to them. She calmly accepts unforeseen changes in her schedule. Although she still has to work harder than most to fit into our socialized society, she behaves, for the most part, like a "normal" eighth grader.

"Oh, Mom," Emily says to me when she is twelve and we discuss her diagnosis, "What is 'normal' anyway? It's just a stereotype. Who wants to live their life as a stereotype?"

Her words have a calming effect on me. I realize that perhaps it is not my vision of parenthood that has been flawed all these years, but my definition of normal. What is normal, anyway?

I have come to learn that normal for me is knowing that some things cannot be changed—only prepared for. Normal is accepting that things don't always turn out the way we thought they would. Uncertainty is normal. Self-doubt is normal. Unpredictability is normal.

For me, living with a child who has Asperger's syndrome is normal.

Jill W. Smith

A Child Like Me

Only another parent can understand that moment of infinite possibilities when the nurse lays your child in your arms for the first time—here's a new life, a new beginning. Perfect in every way, my Anna was nothing like me. She had her mother's blond hair and her own special, indescribable, blue-gray-green eyes. Curling her tiny fingers around my clumsy ones, she looked up at me. Until that moment, I'd never understood that old saying "tug at your heart strings." Now, I promised to teach her, protect her, and most of all, help her avoid all the pain that had dogged my life.

In middle school, I was a bright, chubby child with glasses. A year younger than the kids in my class, I was the perfect victim. I just didn't "get" it—that secret code of childhood. Why were some kids looked up to, fawned on, and followed, while I was scorned and called names? The other boys certainly weren't smarter, and some were even uglier. I studied them on the playground and in the classroom, obsessively trying to learn their secrets. Was it their clothes, the way they talked? There seemed to be no pattern. Some were nice to the other kids; some made fun of them. Some wore the latest fashions, and some wore patches on their clothes. The girls were even more of a mystery, sprouting taller than even the tallest boy; they traveled in packs and giggled behind their hands. The only thing the others seemed to have in common was their contempt for me.

Recess was a gauntlet of jeers and taunts as the other kids passed me over for games and companionship. After five years of that, you'd have thought I would be reconciled to my lonely isolation, my singular social status. But I kept alive my pitiful hopes of acceptance with the knowledge that I had one friend, Jamie, who talked funny because of a cleft palate. As a fellow outcast, I imagined us as the dynamic duo, taking on the bullies of the world, fighting back-to-back with our rapier wit. Of course, I did all the talking.

I look for Jamie the minute I run onto the playground, but Michael grabs me first, hauling on the back of my jacket collar, practically pulling me off me feet. He waves a small envelope in my face.

"Look what I got, Gordo." I hate that nickname, and Michael knows it. Gordo means "fat" in Spanish. "It's an invitation—Jamie's Bar Mitzvah. How many invitations have you got this year?" He already knew.

Early in the year, Rachel, the most popular girl in class, took sneering delight in telling me that none of the kids would invite me to any party because I was "weird"—always talking about my telescopes in a loud voice and correcting the teacher when she gets the facts wrong.

I twist away and stumble across the playground. Michael's laugh echoes in my ears.

"Didja see that? Gordo's so clumsy he tripped over the painted line!"

Blood rushes to my face. "I don't care what that moron thinks. I don't care what that moron thinks," I mutter my mantra as I search for my friend.

Jamie sits alone on the bench by the chain-link fence, his foot swinging in time to a nearby jump rope chant. A gust of wind traps a mud-stained paper against the fence: "C–" it reads. I smile at the thought that it might be Moron Michael's.

Jamie shivers, zips his jacket higher, and turns a forlorn face to me. "Hi, Gordo."

I wince.

"What's up, Jamie?" I sit next to my best friend and spy a small stack of white envelopes in his pocket, like the one Michael just shoved in my face. "Why'd you invite Moron Michael to your Bar Mitzvah?"

"If he comes, the rest of the kids will come too."

"So what if they don't?"

Jamie's pale freckled face gets even paler. "I want kids at my party, not just my baby sister and three cousins."

"I'll be there."

"No." He looks away, past the girls jumping rope.

"Of course, I'll be there! I won't let my best buddy down."

"You're not invited."

I sit there, mouth open and stomach clenched. I heard wrong. Why wouldn't Jamie invite his one and only friend to his party?

"If I invite you the other kids might not come."

I start to breathe again, a long shuddering breath that ends with a sob. The constriction in my stomach moves to my chest and lodges in my throat. I don't say anything, just dash the tears from my eyes and stand up. It's a long walk back to the school building, but I move slowly, not hearing the shrill voices of the other children playing around me, not seeing the muddy piles of snow toppled against the building, not feeling the cold wind lacerate my face and freeze my tears. All I feel is . . . alone. The sense of towering anger and crushing betrayal comes later.

They say time heals all wounds; for me, at least, they scabbed over. I told my parents I didn't want to have a Bar Mitzvah, and they heaved a sigh of relief. In high school, I slimmed down, got contacts, and achieved some measure of belonging with the theater geeks. I even had a date or two.

I found my passion in college—TV journalism. I found my life mate at a singles seminar. I couldn't believe such a pretty, intelligent woman would ever want me, but I bluffed my way through our courtship. We married, built a successful life together, and had a child.

Our daughter, Anna, fulfilled all my expectations and more. She started reading at three and could recite the dialog from any episode of *Thomas the Tank Engine*. She would sit for hours arranging her plastic animals in elaborate patterns. She picked up vocabulary like a sponge, and our friends praised her for being "so adult" in her speech. She was tall and willowy—a lovely, perfect child!

Then I got the call from the nursery school that ripped the scab off my wounds.

"You're daughter seems to be having problems with the other children."

No. It can't be. She's perfect. She's not me. "What kind of problems?"

"She doesn't seem to know how to play with them."

An old, familiar feeling of panic and betrayal roiled my stomach and sent blood pounding to my temples. "Could you give me an example?"

"It's hard to explain; could you and your wife come in for a meeting?"

Dozens of meetings, several doctors, and a disastrous kindergarten year later, we had a name for it: Asperger's syndrome (AS). My daughter suffers from a neurological disorder that impairs her social functioning. She doesn't "get" it—the rules of childhood.

It's genetic.

I embarked on a desperate odyssey, learning everything I could about AS—how to treat it, how to value its strengths, how to help children compensate for their social impairment. Like many of the children that manifest the "little professor syndrome," Anna is exceptionally bright but physically clumsy; she has narrow and passionate interests, and she has no clue on how to get along with her peers. In the past, children with this disorder limped through childhood misdiagnosed, ridiculed, and isolated. The lucky ones—like me—had supportive families and trained their intellect to acquire social skills so they could "pass" in normal society. Others found some special niche where they became harmless eccentrics or valued "absent-minded professors." The less lucky ones obsessed over Star Trek or bus schedules and lived in their parents' basements, eking out a living with low-level jobs that didn't require contact with the public.

Now in sixth grade, Anna has occupational therapy, physical therapy, social skills training, and a special school where she is valued for what she can do, not ridiculed for what she can't. She has real friends whom she chats with on the phone and who come over for play dates and sleepovers. She's invited to all the kids' parties.

Most of all, Anna has a father who's been there, who understands and can help her deal with the pain of being different. So I still hope to fulfill my parental promise to teach and protect. I fervently believe Anna will be smarter, stronger, and much happier than I ever was as a child.

During this family crisis, I faced my worst fear— having a child like me—and realized that to love her fully, I have to love those aspects of myself that give me pain. With that love came self-forgiveness and understanding. Looking back, I wouldn't change myself or my daughter—just the world that doesn't value our differences or see our strengths.

F. L. Justice, as told by Anna's father, G. L. Stein

Good Marching

"Way down yonder where the dolphins play . . ."

Raffi's mellow voice floats from the den into the kitchen as I make my list of groceries. Pasta and eggs, bagels, another box of the cinnamon cereal Daniel will usually tolerate. Bread, ketchup, and apple juice, of course. Knowing I've forgotten something, I take another glance through my small pantry, and then steal a glance out the window. The gray sky warns of snow, and I hope to complete my shopping before the roads get slick.

". . . the waves come in and the waves go out . . ."

I know by heart these songs by this popular children's singer I never knew existed before my daughter was born. I sing along with the refrain in my head in spite of myself, "Baby beluga, baby beluga." Natalie's earnest six-year-old voice rises above the sound of the music as I review my spices.

"That's a whale, Daniel. Belugas are whales. I like whales, Daniel. Whales are big."

My children are watching the same video they've watched countless times before. My son has certain favorites of which he never grows weary. My daughter, older by two years and wiser by ages, doesn't seem to mind. She accepts his idiosyncrasies and watches with him.

"Whales live in the ocean, Daniel. Do you like the ocean?"

There is no reply to her question. There is never any reply.

My son was two years old when his team of therapists told me he had autism. I drove home that day blinded by confusion and fear, for I understood very little then of this disorder I would eventually come to know so intimately. Back then I had only a vague awareness of this pervasive, developmental disorder, which I had gleaned largely from the movie *Rain Man*. My ignorance was that of a woman who had never seriously considered that such a tragedy could touch her life.

Glancing at Daniel's reflection in his car seat through my rearview mirror as I drove, I felt again the familiar ache as he gazed out the window, his impassive, beautiful face giving no hint at what was happening in his mind. Turning onto Sheridan Road, I realized I was crying, quietly at first, and then sobbing so violently I had to pull the car over to the side of the road. I didn't know much about autism then, not much at all. But I knew enough to recognize that my life would never be the same.

In the weeks and months to come, I moved in a daze, a wall of insulating denial protectively surrounding my consciousness. Numbly following the advice of experts at Northwestern University, I enrolled Daniel in numerous therapies. We practiced painstaking exercises with him at home, read materials our neurologist provided, and sought books and articles from the library. But in those early days, I didn't fully comprehend the profound and far-reaching nature of this disorder. In my naiveté, I actually questioned aloud if Daniel's condition would affect his sister, Natalie. Over time, of course, the question became, "How could this not affect Natalie?" . . . or, indeed, any of us.

Even as I drove my son to therapies designed to engage him in our world, my world was shrinking to the inescapable truth that his life, our lives, were irreparably altered. As one therapist carelessly told me, "He'll never be normal." The bright, unencumbered future I had imagined for us had suddenly dissolved into threatening uncertainty.

Raffi is singing now of children around the world: "Achmed lives in Egypt, José lives in Peru . . ."

I picture Natalie on the sofa, her small legs straight in front of her, balancing a coloring book on her lap. Daniel will be standing in front of the television, his stocking feet pounding along the stretch of wooden floor where the carpet ends. He seems to enjoy this repetitive motion. We believe the noise, pressure, and stimulation of marching this way somehow comforts him, allowing him to relate better to his physical world. The noise no longer bothers me; I barely even hear it.

"And each one is much like the other . . . a lot like me and you." The first flakes of snow are falling now as I complete my grocery list, and I feel a stab of anxiety. I no longer enjoy the snow, no longer appreciate its serene beauty as it coats the branches of the apple tree outside my kitchen window. I fear its hidden dangers—the icy patch lurking on the road's surface, waiting to catch me unaware, sending me careening out of control.

"You're my brother, Daniel," my daughter explains gently. "I'm glad you are my brother."

She couldn't wait for the birth of her new sibling, whom she breathlessly referred to throughout my pregnancy as "the new baby." But once he arrived and began to grow, Natalie's eagerly anticipated new brother proved bafflingly unwilling to engage. The typical sibling game playing and reciprocity that she had so looked forward to did not emerge as he matured into a toddler. Daniel showed no interest in patty cake, playing catch, or even sharing reading time as we curled together in bed each evening. Most content when left alone, he existed, seemingly happy, sheltered in his own mysterious world. Occasionally he would show mild interest in our dog, a young Sheltie, intrigued, perhaps, by her constant motion or stimulated by the feel of her fur beneath his fingers. Natalie's enthusiastic invitations to play, however, were almost wholly rebuffed, her effort to be the encouraging, hands-on big sister she longed to be thwarted on a daily basis.

In the darkest part of night, as sleep eluded me, I'd despair at this unwelcome path we now had to follow, grieving all that should have been for my son and for my daughter. I questioned whether I could do it, whether I had the courage to meet the challenge of this unusual boy, whether I would survive the heartbreak that seemed to pervade each day.

"I'm lost here, God," I'd whisper in the dark. "I don't know how to do this."

Tucking my grocery list in my purse, I hurry to the den and tell Natalie I'm going to change clothes. "We'll get our shopping done extra quickly today, okay?"

"Okay, Mommy," she replies, glancing up from her coloring with her wistful smile as I head quickly upstairs.

The thump, thump, thump of Daniel's stomping follows me, muted now as I change from old sweats to a pair of jeans. Vaguely, I realize how often this sound fills our home, this strange marching that communicates nothing to us as we listen, watching and hoping for a sign. It occurs to me as I check my lipstick that at least when I hear him stomping I know what he is up to, saving me from investigating an even more troubling silence.

The video has come to an end, and the applause of the audience drifts up the stairs. *Good timing,* I think.

Then Natalie's voice reaches me again, tireless in her effort to engage this oddly behaving boy, so different from what she had expected, to draw him close, to share her love in a way he will understand.

"Good marching, Daniel!" she praises him proudly. "You're good at marching!"

Again, he doesn't respond, but I doubt I would hear him if he did. I stand absolutely still, as the blood rushes to my face, and I feel my heartbeat pulsing at my temple. I stare, motionless, at my reflection in the mirror, the tube of lipstick halfway to my lips.

"Good marching, Daniel," I murmur to myself. "Good marching . . ." Slowly I begin to smile. "Yes, my beautiful boy, you're good at marching."

We'll start with that.

Thank you, Natalie.

She is standing at the window as I return to the den and turns to me with delight. "It's snowing, Mommy!" she tells me, her eyes eager and glowing. "Can we play in the snow?"

I kneel and pull her close, breathe in her sweet child smell, my lips trembling against her hair. Reaching out to catch Daniel in our embrace, I hold them tightly for a moment, their sturdy bodies warm against my chest.

"Yes, sweetheart," I say softly. "We can play in the snow. Let's go marching in the snow."

Kristen M. Scott

Arms Wide Open

I envy Barbie. With a quick trip to her closet, she can change her profession with a new set of clothes. She can be Astronaut Barbie, Ballerina Barbie, even Marine Corps Sergeant Barbie! But not Mommy Barbie. That job is left to Midge, her mousy-haired friend. When I floundered into the realm of parenting a child with special needs, I learned the secret of why Barbie could be over ninety professions, but never a mom.

At age four, my son Henry was verbal but often flapped his arms, covered his ears, and avoided eye contact. In the manner of Mommy Detective, I asked his teachers and pediatrician: "Did they maybe notice anything wrong?" (*Please say no.*)

This is difficult for me to admit, but not only did I want a normal child, I wanted an exceptional child. I wanted a child people would look at, marvel at, and then look to me and say, "What a wonderful job you've done." Embarrassingly, this fantasy extended further to experts questioning me, wanting to learn my parenting wisdom.

So, I was greatly relieved when both his teacher and doctor reported they'd never noticed anything wrong. I blissfully assumed Henry would outgrow his unusual behaviors, oblivious to the iceberg in my shipping lane.

In Henry's preschool class that year was a child with special needs, Matthew. Occasionally, Matthew's case worker observed him in class. After a visit, she told a teacher she'd "noticed some issues with that boy," and pointed toward Henry. "Are his parents aware of them?" Henry's teacher told me this as we stood outside his classroom in a hall crowded with parents dropping off children and chatting.

"You told her the doctor said he was fine, right?" I asked nervously.

"Yes, but . . . she said pediatricians aren't experts in this field and that you need to get Henry evaluated."

My heart froze. "I don't understand. What did she mean?"

"She thinks something's wrong with him," she said and looked down.

At that moment, in that crowded hall in the middle of winter, the flood gates opened and swept away the last of my denial. A hot flush spread over me. I buried my face in my hands and cried. Like a child on the first day of kindergarten who doesn't want Mother to leave, I sobbed great gulping sobs.

I felt a gentle pat on my shoulder and heard a mumbled, "I'm sorry, I have to go back in the class-room."

I was dimly aware of a settling hush in the cor-ridor and the other parents' stares. I couldn't blame the teacher for hightailing it out of the hall. I didn't want to be there either, but I couldn't move. And I couldn't stop crying.

All my fears collided. Would other kids make fun of Henry? Would he have to ride the "special" bus? Would he be able to get a job someday? Would he get worse? Was it my fault?

It took four long months to get an evaluation appointment. Four months of vacillating between thoughts of *Maybe there's nothing wrong* and *Oh, God, what could it be?*

Finally the day arrived. I dressed in my Sunday best, wearing my shiny new clothes like armor. I wet Henry's curly hair and smoothed it down. As we drove up to the imposing hospital on the hill, my stomach clenched.

Over the course of four hours, Henry underwent testing and evaluations by a team that included a devel-opmental pediatrician, a social worker, a speech pathol-ogist, an audiologist, and an occupational therapist.

Worried about the deep psychological toll the testing would take on my son, I wrung my hands and wished I owned a Guatemalan worry doll. But Henry surprised me as we waited for the results by saying, "That was more fun than I thought it would be."

When the social worker called me into her office, I left Henry with my mother and walked as if going to a court sentencing.

"We are leaning towards sensory integration disorder or borderline Asperger's. Both are on the autism spectrum," she said.

I didn't cry. My new job as Henry's personal, take-no-shit, advocate didn't allow for tears. Instead, I imagined a color spectrum with autistic disorders as the primary colors. I wondered what shade Henry was.

"He tested in the lower one-hundred-fifties for IQ," she said.

"Great! Does that mean he's a genius?" I leaned forward.

"Yes, although we don't like to use labels like that."

Go ahead, label my son a genius! I really don't mind, I thought.

She knit her brow and tapped her yellow pencil. "His fine motor skills tested in the low eighties."

"So he's a genius who can't write?" I said. "He's a genius!" I sang in my mind.

"Anytime there is more than fifteen points of deviation, we're concerned. Henry deviated by nearly seventy points."

Deviations? Points? That didn't sound good. I wanted to go back to the genius part and tried to control the feeling that I was gasping for air from the depths of the ocean.

"We're recommending occupational therapy," she said.

"But he doesn't have a job," I joked.

She didn't laugh.

"Occupational therapy helps kids in their jobs of playing and learning."

"Will this fix him?"

She looked at me as though I were wearing a bathing suit in church. "Therapy will help him with proprioceptive grading, regulating his sensory intake, and his fine motor skills. Oh, and you may want to have him fitted for musician's earplugs to use occasionally, like in noisy restaurants."

Too embarrassed to admit I didn't understand all the words, I pretended I did.

The next week Henry began working with a wonderful occupational therapist. Although his motor skills slowly improved, his flapping became worse at times. We would be in line at the grocery store and he would start flapping, sometimes emitting small noises. When people stared, I tried to suppress the embarrassed, panicky feelings and to channel my inner mother bear—but mustered only an inner squirrel.

Not confident I was doing enough, I decided a full tactical assault was called for and made appointments with various specialists. The first doctor, a supposed expert in autism spectrum disorders, barely glanced at Henry and recommended Ritalin. Next, I took him to a neurologist, who claimed Henry had Tourette's syndrome. Hoping for an easy cure, I asked about treatments. With his soothing Indian accent, his voice riding up and down over the words, he said, "Unless symptoms are severe—say, interrupting his education—there is nothing we can do."

I had Henry tested for mercury, allergies, the works. I put him on a gluten-free diet and gave him supplements and homeopathic remedies. I even visited a psychic. She said, "He'll outgrow it," and then handed me a bill for $150. Nothing changed Henry's behavior.

At the height of my answer-searching frenzy, I went to a party given by a neighbor, Molly. Her husband was a Nike executive, and most of the other people at the party were Nike men and their wives, all extremely fit and lovely in their high-performance spandex.

During cocktails, Molly pulled me aside. "I want to introduce you to Anna." Her eyes scanned the

room while I imagined why she would want to introduce us. *Perhaps Anna needed some tips on how to
exercise less and eat more?* Most of the women there
looked like they could use a sandwich. Or two.

Molly turned to me and sighed. "I don't see her,
but when I find her I'll bring her over."

"Sure, I'd love to meet her," I said in my any-
friend-of-yours-is-a-friend-of-mine voice.

She touched my arm. "I think it would be super
if you two could talk."

"Okay . . . why's that?" I said.

"Her son has something wrong with him, too,"
she said blithely and floated away.

*"Wrong with him?" Is that the way I represented
Henry to the world?* I pushed that thought out of my
mind and focused instead on sharp replies I could
have said to Molly. Ruminating on what I could've
said after the moment has passed is somewhat of
a hobby of mine or at least something I often find
myself doing.

Her Ken doll husband walked up, put his mus-
cular arm around me, and squeezed. Nearly blinded
by his brilliant white teeth, I squinted and smiled up
at him.

"Molly told me about Henry. How arrrrre you?"
His cashmere brown eyes were full of sympathy and
something else, a look of *Thank God it's your kid and
not mine.* This nudged me over the edge. In the free

fall, I saw how much I wanted to be like these people with their perfect bodies and normal kids.

I hated him; I hated Molly.

But most of all, I hated myself.

I saw Henry as someone who needed to be fixed, and by golly, wasn't it my job to do it?

No. I was focusing on the wrong color in Henry's rainbow. That night, I quit the job of fixing my son.

There is one thing that didn't show up on any of Henry's tests, one thing that I overlooked because I was so focused on finding solutions: his loving heart.

When he was five, Henry came home from preschool and announced proudly, "Mom, I was a hero today!" He explained how he saw an older boy picking on a girl at recess while other kids watched. Henry walked up to the boy and told him to stop.

"And he did, Mom, He stopped!" Henry said, adding, "Then he punched me in the stomach. Pow!"

Once I stopped being on high alert for atypical behaviors, I started noticing how my son looks out for the younger kids at the playground, the patience he shows with his senile great-grandparents, and how he saves even the smallest spider from being stepped on. I realized that he has the biggest heart of any person I've ever met.

We still go to occupational therapy, but I've taken a new job—to be the one person Henry can count on to love him exactly as he is.

So just in case a Mattel executive is reading this and wants to know how to make a Mommy Barbie, I've got some ideas. First, keep the ginormous breasts; they'd be handy for nursing. But take Barbie off her tiptoes and widen her stance a little; she needs to have the soles of her feet firmly on the ground. Finally, and this is most important of all, you need to change her arms. Instead of stiff arms that only rise up and down, she needs the flexibility to throw them wide open.

Tiffany Talbott

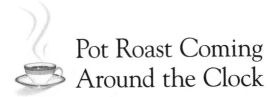

Pot Roast Coming Around the Clock

I watch from the family room as my tall, thin, twenty-eight-year-old son David stands in the kitchen and follows a familiar ritual. His back to me, he writes in the air with a blue pen an inch from the ivy wallpaper.

On his left is a wall calendar with a garden picture and my own scribbled notes: *10:30, Dr. Green; 12:30, lunch with Susan; 7:00, Edwards Board meeting.* With its grid of white squares, wood frame, and surrounding ivy, this calendar resembles a trellis holding the details of my life. Standing next to it, David seems sadly in its margins and more than a little strange.

I slip an entry into my journal about his baffling behavior. I hope an accumulation of such notes will help me understand my son and his unique way of seeing the world. The threads are as mysterious as David's writing in the air. Most puzzling of all are the entries about time.

Five years ago, David was sitting in the kitchen while I fixed dinner. He kept asking, "Dinner will be soon?" Suddenly he proclaimed, "Pot roast coming around the clock." I stopped chopping onions and looked at him. He seemed to see a pot roast riding on our clock's hands instead of simmering in the oven.

Of course, this is how his life goes, I thought, *food and services delivered to him.* Much of his life is spent waiting—waiting for the lift bus to take him to work or bring him home, waiting for park district day trips to the beach or Mt. Hood, waiting for dinner. Waiting slows down time.

But the image of the clock as a deliverer of objects may also explain why he thinks he can repair a music tape he's hopelessly tangled or make wilted daisies raise their heads again. "They'll drink the water; they'll be okay," he says. If objects are pinned like donkey tails to a clock's hands, surely they will come around again.

I wish I had realized when David was younger how much he needed objects and ritual to help him navigate time. When he was five, he cried, "No, no!" each time I removed an ornament from the Christmas tree. Frantically, he tried to return the ornament to its branch. I began to remove holiday decorations when he was not around.

Three years ago, I heard him chant, "Gingerbread house teapot, put away. Christmas is all finished." He carried our ceramic teapot from the kitchen to a hall cupboard. After years of frustration, he had learned to use an object to mark the end of the holiday season.

When he was growing up, David also insisted on leaving his empty Easter basket next to his bed all year. Now I think that he wanted to make sure Easter would return.

He left his little boy shin guards on his dresser until he was twenty-five, perhaps hoping to play soccer again. When he was twelve, a coach had made him feel he could play the game. In reality, all he could do was kick the ball down the field and shoot it into the net. He could not watch other players and synchronize his actions with theirs. As he got older, there was no appropriate team for him, even in Special Olympics. But his hopes, attached to yellow shin guards, did not change.

For years, David has had an obsession with wall calendars and schedules. He pats them, arranges their pages, and presses them against the wall. Sometimes, as I described earlier, he writes in the air next to them. By these actions, he may be showing his need for a tangible symbol of time.

To some extent, this need is universal. When we remodeled our kitchen a few years ago, I was disoriented when both the clock and calendar were removed. Though I was still able to function, I was relieved when they were finally put back on our repapered walls. Since then, I've tried to move the calendar to our office and the clock to a different wall, but David moves them back to their former positions. His need for pattern exceeds mine.

Even more than most children, David loved repetition. When he was four, he pushed his rubber duck off the bathtub rim into the water again and again, each time crowing "Poor dut." Like a baby playing peek-a-boo, he was learning that events can create a pattern.

Eight years ago, the workshop where he performed packaging jobs lost contracts. With time to fill, he roamed the building. At home, he repeated staff and coworkers' admonitions: "Be quiet! Go to your work station!"

Alarming reports peppered our mail: "Thirty-two incidents of verbal disruption and wandering." "Crossed Alexander Street to throw paper over a fence. Nearly hit by a car." "We found David hanging from the awning outside the building."

One day after the bus dropped David off at our house, I heard him say, "Hush up, be quiet! . . . I will be quiet." Like Golum in *The Lord of the Rings*, he struggled between opposing voices.

Sensing his frustration, I went to sit next to him on the sofa in the living room. "Is all that talking in there bothering you?" I asked, pointing to my own head.

Cupping his hand over the left side of my head, he said, "Yeah."

As David became more absorbed in self-talk, he seemed to grow increasingly out of touch with himself and out of sync with time. After one particularly long, rambling speech, he said, "I will be quiet. I'll be quiet forever." Certainly this was not what we wanted.

His anxiety high, he was more obsessed than ever about the wall calendar in the hallway at work. A supervisor told me that after the old page was ripped off each month, David frantically sifted through the trash, found the page, and taped it back. It seemed he could maintain a slight degree of control only if time were whole.

In a journal entry on April 17, 1997, I wrote: *David still will not allow the calendar page at home to remain on April. "It's still March!" he insists. Does he want to stop time—to keep the past in the past and the future in the future?*

The workshop staff tried using a concrete calendar to help him cope with changes in his schedule. In a four-part sequence, the first picture showed David hanging up his coat and putting away his lunch; the second showed his morning work task; the third, his break time; and the fourth, his afternoon work task. He was supposed to turn each picture over after he completed the activity.

But familiar patterns had been hopelessly broken. Finally, we arranged for him to move to another work program. With a more consistent schedule, more understanding staff, and a mood-stabilizing medication, he became calmer and less obsessed by the calendar.

David's anxiety about time stems from autism, rapid cycle bi-polar disorder, and obsessive compulsive disorder, but also, I think, partly from the nature of time itself.

The flow of time can be confusing even to those who do not have autism. The clock suggests a cyclical movement, as reflected in David's image of pot roast circling it. But the calendar shows linear movement, even though days, weeks, months, and seasons repeat. Time sometimes seems to have a vertical movement, suggested by the expression "sand through an hourglass."

The calendar also promises a stillness and control it does not deliver, much to David's distress. Its boxes, lined up like soldiers, suggest that days, weeks, and months are separate—even equal. Yet we know that past, present, and future flow together. And time does not march steadily forward; instead, it lurches or languishes, staggers and falls back. In reality, time is not a soldier but a mercurial phantom.

To cope with these contradictions, we use symbols and ceremonies. We mark the beginning of summer with a barbecue, the end of our workday with a happy hour or tea time. We celebrate a birthday or wedding with a cake and a memorial service with flowers. Symbols give our lives meaning and help us to go on. We learn to root ourselves in time.

Being rooted in time is difficult for someone who has autism, but easier when time is tied to objects and when events have a perceivable pattern. When I talk to David about an upcoming activity, I try to say the day of the month and point to it on the calendar.

David's language reflects his confusion about time. Describing his work week, David once remarked, "Friday you get down to home." He says, "I'll go to work today-tomorrow," showing he's not sure when one day becomes the next. He doesn't try to tell time on the clock, and he doesn't say an event will happen next month or next year. But he is making progress in talking about time.

On vacation in Sunriver, Oregon, last summer, I rewound the movie we had just watched and put it back in its plastic case.

"Will we take the movie tapes back to the store?" David asked.

"Yes," I told him.

Then, pressing for more information, he said, "When will we take them back?" His voice, though still somewhat flat, like Dustin Hoffman's in *Rain Man*, lifted slightly at the end. For the first time, he had used the word "when."

Writing about David during the past few years, I've realized he has given me the gift of seeing time in a new way. Without his strange behavior of writing in the air, I would not have pictured the calendar as a trellis that provides support. It does not force us into a particular shape, but allows us to find our own pattern.

At thirty-four, David's personhood is still unfolding. Although he doesn't play soccer as he'd hoped, he does bowl and cross-country ski. He has a large case filled with Special Olympics medals. And he writes upcoming activities on a calendar in his own room. He derives time's meaning from objects, such as pot roast and the gingerbread house teapot, and from familiar patterns—as I do.

It isn't important that he knows how to tell the hours and minutes. Others will do this for him. What is important is that he learns to live in the present, unhindered by regrets for his past and fears for his future.

Phyllis Mannan

Escalatorland

Will is turning six, and I'm getting pretty excited about this year's birthday cake. I think I've figured out how to do it: I'll start with a pound cake, and slant it somehow, and then start carving. Silver food coloring? They must sell it somewhere. And black licorice for the rails. And a new comb to make grooves in the frosting. And, oh yes, a red gumdrop for the emergency button. And . . . my God, it's happened. I've gone insane. I've joined my son in Escalatorland.

Who would've guessed that when I decided it was finally time for Will to choose his own birthday party theme that I'd be the one to get so into it? In the past, I had always been the theme thruster—pushing Pooh, touting Thomas, strong-arming Sesame Street, as Will went cheerfully along with the flow. Now, out of courtesy and respect for my growing son, I asked what he wanted, and out popped the concept for which neither Hallmark nor Disney could provide any assistance whatsoever: an escalator party.

It's interesting to me that I so quickly accepted this vision, considering the fact that I once despised the big rolling monsters. After a lifetime of barely noticing them, escalators suddenly began to loom large in my parenting life because they possess the power to take my child's mind away from anything a kid would normally love. Up and up we'd go, whenever the people-carrying machine appeared before us. Away from the world, we'd float—past the F.A.O. Schwartz windows gleaming with DayGlo; up and beyond the colorful garden of kiddie books at Barnes and Noble; up, up, and into oblivion, leaving behind the ice cream, the popcorn, the clowns, and balloons in the Seattle Center Food Circus. All the wonders of childhood disappeared below as we continued our slow, steady ascent to nowhere.

From the time Will was two, nothing could attract him like the magical motorized staircase. Like Richard Dreyfuss moving toward the mother ship as the *Close Encounters* theme chimed, Will would see the shining steps and head for outer space. Of course, I knew I was riding on the wheels of controversy: Should the parents and therapists of these small addicts let them have their fixations and try to use the deified item as a learning tool, as some professionals in the world of autism advise? Or should we force the children, in a different form of therapy, to go cold turkey and strictly point them in another direction? Kids like mine take their narrow interests to the bizarre extreme; they so deftly find a way to block out the real world. When you find yourself walking through life hand-in-hand with one of them, their single-mindedness takes you by surprise and leaves you anxiously wondering which way to pull. If possible, I try to yank him away and turn him around, but his determination and rigidity can make this a superhuman task, and many attempts have failed to distract him.

One day as my son and I stood perched at the top of yet another landing, with Will jumping and flapping as excitedly as a climber who'd reached the summit of Everest, I knelt at his side in desperation. "Will!" I implored in a harsh whisper, gripping his little arm. "There's more to life than escalators!"

He just took my hand and stepped on, and by the time we'd arrived at the next floor of that particular department store, he was crowing to the shoppers at top volume: "There's more to life than escalators! There's more to life than escalators!"

As folks peered over at us with curious expressions, I began to dream of automatic stairs that could lift me through the roof—up, up, and away.

Eventually, though, I began to understand the escalators' calming effect. When the stress of life becomes too much, as it does each day for Will, wouldn't I, too, seek out the hypnotic release of the Pacific Ocean if I saw that it were available in every downtown bank building? Will had found the relaxation method that was perfect in every way for him. It never changed. It couldn't come at you from left field—like nature or a human. If there was an up one, there was a down one; and if there was a down one, there was an up one. The symmetry and regularity could be challenged only in the event of a power outage or if somebody got their shoestring caught.

So in the most child-centered style of surrender, I literally went along for the ride. Through department stores and office buildings, hotels and hospitals, shopping malls and airports and bus tunnels, we blazed our vertical trail. I tried my best to educate along the way. We noticed skylights above our heads, babies riding with us, numbers and letters that marked our path. But somewhere between floors, my pedagogical stance got wiped out. I found myself wondering about the escalator's innards (which we once got to glimpse during a thrilling moment with repairmen at a local hospital), its history (who invented it? In what year?), and its manufacturers (Otis and Haughton are two proud names one often sees engraved at the foot). I imagined the Midwestern escalator factory we might one day visit in a distant berg, like Oshkosh or Fargo. I even pictured mother and son getting together to beat a Guinness record—so many escalators in so many days in so many cities. The two of us, weary but grinning for the media, at the last plateau in some super mall in Canada.

So the birthday cake is, to me, a monument to our travels—though, when I come back down to Earth, I suppose I'll think of it as a milestone to build and leave behind. After all, you might be thinking, there's got to be a way for William and his mom to get over this, or at least branch out.

I thought of a new title for Will's celebration, and it seems to check out okay with him—Things That Go Up and Down. This way, in addition to the original and amazing cake, we can include yo-yos, bouncing balls, and swings, to the relief of our party guests, no doubt. And perhaps these variations on a theme will allow my little guy to one day see that, like the waves that roll up and hit the sand, like the sun that rises and sets, in the scheme of things, there's more to life than escalators.

Kelly Harland

Learning to Talk

I crouch over Elliot's small body, kneeling in the stinking mess on the floor and not caring a bit. All that matters is pulling my son close to me. I'm crying as I fuss over his rigid limbs, try to ease his hands off his ears with kisses, and attempt to quiet the animal shrieking with butterfly fingers across his lips.

It doesn't work, of course; the closeness is for my sake. I know that, but I can't help myself. It's a primal thing, a maternal thing. I am reminded of a photograph in a newspaper—another woman, a mother, clad in full burqa, crouching over her child, shielding the small body with her own from the bullets flying in that far-away street.

I wish with all my heart that I could protect my child as that woman had. But I am not enough. My ample, un-toned flesh cannot block out the angry shouting and the crowd of staring faces that have surrounded us. And now my cuddles are only adding to Elliot's panic. If my husband, Lee, were here, he would know how to handle this. Always calm, always in control, he would have protected us both. But he had gone away to defend women and children like the ones in the newspaper and never came back, and I feel alone on the sticky floor of the supermarket sweets aisle. Outraged voices scorch the air, terrifying my son and burning me deeply.

"It's a disgrace, that's what it is! She's crying, but who's gonna have to clean up? Me, that's who!"

"Child's more animal than human, should be in a home or something."

"Someone should help her!"

"What's going on?"

"Disgrace, I tell ya! He only went and peed in the pick 'n mix. Just lifted the lid and let rip all over the sherbets!"

"Wouldn't have happened in my day!"

"People that can't control their kids shouldn't have them. It's a disgrace!"

I carry a card in my bag for situations like this. It explains in simple language how Elliot's autism can affect him and requests politely that if I'm left to deal with him, everything will be okay shortly. My card speaks for me when my throat is tight with tears, when I want to shout back, to swear and throw punches—except that I can't see my bag anywhere among the milling feet. And I have to get these people to shut up and go away right now, or it'll be hours before I can calm Elliot.

"Please, be quiet." My voice surprises me with its smallness. "Leave us alone. You're scaring him. He wasn't being naughty; to him, if it has a lid, it must be a toilet."

No one listens. My words are lost in the excited babble. I look up at the ring of gawking faces, mouths open, tongues flapping, minds closed, and I feel a moment of real closeness to my poor frightened son.

"My son is mentally disabled." I don't shout, but my words explode into the crowd and silence the onlookers. After a few seconds of deafening silence, the people begin to drift away, like smoke. Even the puffed-up shop assistant backs off, muttering, "Shouldn't be allowed around normal people then. Disgrace!"

I ignore them all. Insults, like hastily mumbled apologies, are only wisps of air. Even the way the crowd backs off, as if my beautiful son were infectious, is nothing to me now.

During the five years since the diagnosis that changed our world, Elliot and I have both been learning to talk. His few words are all the more valuable for being so rare, and I have learned to say "autism" and "disability" without flinching. I have acquired polite phrases that I can trot out whenever I need the world to give my son a break. I have excuses for shop assistants, irritated because Elliot has organized their produce into perfect symmetry. I have explanations for the angry motorist whose car Elliot is licking because it is red. I have words to calm the frightened mothers in the playground when they look like they want to form a lynch mob because Elliot's clumsy attempts to communicate have made their children cry. I can now be composed as I excuse my precious boy; but, oh my, it's been a long, hard journey.

A baby learns to talk by copying. He will stare for hours at his mother's face, watching the shape of her mouth and her many expressions. He will mimic simple vowel sounds and eventually practice the music of speech with repeated nursery rhymes. Now, what about the child who can't look at faces? The child who cries and covers his ears when anyone sings, because any discord is physically painful to them? What about the child who finds the discrepancies between our words and our body language to be aversive? How much more wonderful when that child learns to speak! What marvelous things they might have to say! These muted voices deserve our attention.

The aisle is quiet and still now. After a while, Elliot's wailing dwindles to sobs. I sit beside him and watch as the stiffness leaves his body and his eyes open. When he's ready, I pull him onto my lap and hand him the red woolen hat I keep in my pocket. He rolls it onto his head and down over his face. And there we sit: Elliot in his world of blank redness and me, singing softly. "Old MacDonald had a farm, e-i-e-i-o / and on that farm he had an elephant, e-i-e-i-o." We're up to gorillas when a tiny voice issues from the hat. "Lowland or forest?"

I smile as I ask, "Sorry, honey, what did you say?"

The hat lifts a fraction. "Lowland or forest?"

"Ooops! Lowland, definitely." I sing another verse and then ask, "Are you ready to go home now?"

He doesn't say anything but stands up and waits while I struggle to my feet, retrieve my bag, and use a handful of wipes to get the worst of the smelly mess off my skirt. I know that Elliot can see perfectly well through the wool of his "safety" hat, so I don't attempt to hold his hand. I abandon the shopping trolley and follow him out of the shop, admiring as always the efficient way he weaves through the crowds to avoid touching anyone.

Someone once commented that I must wish that things were different. "Yes," I agreed, "I suppose I must. I wish I were a few pounds lighter; I wish I had more money. But I wouldn't change Elliot for the world, and the world is a better place with him in it." I recall this conversation as Elliot and I negotiate the newspaper stand by the exit. The word "autism" howls at me from the headlines. Apparently, advances are being made in prenatal testing. Doctors are hoping to be able to formulate a test for autism, so couples can choose to abort a disabled fetus.

Despite myself, I move closer to Elliot, my hand hovering near his head, just short of stroking his golden hair. "Hoping"—what a word to use in such a context. Elliot and his friends are not mistakes, not normal children gone wrong. They love, laugh, and know joy, and they are a joy to know. Elliot doesn't squabble or whine or sulk, and he will never learn to lie. He certainly has his fair share of challenging behavior, but I think we could all learn a lot from this special, gentle boy who looks at the world from a different angle.

It's raining outside, and a rank full of taxis wait invitingly to our left. I hesitate before following Elliot to the right, along the main street toward the train station. The rain feels nice on my hot cheeks, and I'm in no mood, anyway, for a repeat of the time Elliot tried to climb out of a taxi window as we sped home because the driver was whistling.

When the doctors diagnose your child with autism, they offer you lots of homilies and advice to help you come to terms with the sudden change of direction. I was told that God only gives special children to special people. (I didn't know whether to laugh or cry at that.) I was given the analogy of pregnancy being like a plane journey, a carefully planned expedition to the sunny Caribbean. You've read the brochures, your friends have all been there, and you know what to expect. But when your plane lands—when your special child is born—you find yourself in Belgium. It's not what you wanted, for sure, but, you are told, when you get used to it, you'll find it interesting and fun.

Rubbish! I think to myself as I tag along behind Elliot, wishing he wanted to splash in the puddles. *It's more like landing on the moon with neither luggage nor gravity boots.*

The moment we enter the train station, Elliot is happier. The hat comes off. I push it back into my pocket for next time. Elliot strokes his ticket, enjoying the smooth, shiny texture. He laughs aloud with pure delight to see it sucked in and then spat out by the automatic gates. We go back and do it again eight times, until the lure of the trains is too much for him, and we can head out onto the platform. Fortunately, the guard is familiar with this routine and smiles at us indulgently.

We choose a bench, a red one, of course, and sit down. Railway platforms aren't usually thought of as peaceful places, but that's exactly how I'm feeling now—peaceful. The colorful hanging baskets sparkle with wet begonias, and my son is smiling. I inch a bit closer to him, and he doesn't move away. A fast train roars through on the opposite track. I'm amazed, as always, that such a loud noise doesn't bother Elliot at all while a popping balloon or a baby crying can set him trembling and wild-eyed. As the roar passes into the distance, I realize Elliot is speaking.

". . . can achieve an average speed of ninety miles per hour, while some high-speed trains can reach speeds in excess of 120 miles per hour. The cheetah is the fastest land animal, and it can run at seventy miles per hour, while it's usual prey, the zebra, can run at forty miles per hour. . . ."

He's a marvel, my son. I adore every weird and wonderful ounce of him. I have run the gamut of emotions and come out smiling. I think briefly of the angry sweets lady back at the shop. I'll bet she doesn't know how fast a cheetah can run!

Jennifer Casey

Life with the Family Gangsta

Sometimes, you just have to laugh. As the father and primary caregiver of a young man with autism, I've learned over the years that laughter can be a way to cope with difficult times. The ability to find humor in offbeat moments, to laugh at funny experiences, can soothe the weary soul and release the stress that comes from living every day with autism. At times, it seems the only thing that keeps me afloat and carries us into the future is humor.

Caring for my twenty-four-year-old son, Sam, has given me an ironic perspective on life. Words like "proper" and "normal" no longer mean much to me, not when the head banging starts anyway. I don't mean to make light of the situation or to diminish the difficult times that come all too frequently, but I've earned my right to be sardonic. I've been punched, kicked, scratched, and bit. I've been pushed down stairs and shoved into walls. One day I suffered the indignity of being chased around my front yard by my broom-wielding son in full view of our neighbors. *Ha ha ha! It's just Sam having a bad moment. Not to worry, really. He'll calm down in a minute or two.*

No question, Sam can be difficult. Yet, on other occasions he can be absolutely delightful—a joy to have as a life companion. Let me give you an example. First, though, I need to introduce Sam: At five feet, eight inches, he's a stocky 190 pounds with a more or less neatly trimmed beard and curly brown hair tucked under a baseball cap. He lives semi-independently in a fully equipped apartment in our basement, dubbed the "Yellow Submarine" after its sunny yellow paint and a poster of the Beatles' movie of the same name hanging on the wall. His three other caregivers, all males, spend time in Sam's bachelor pad and take him out to movies and restaurants.

Unlike many people on the autism spectrum, Sam chatters nonstop, usually about his two favorite topics. His current obsessions are weather, especially tornadoes, and rap music, courtesy of his youngest caregiver, who introduced Sam to the likes of Snoop Dogg, Outkast, Ludacris, 50 Cent, and Jurassic 5.

So now Sam comes hip-hopping down the hallway, singing along with his walkman: "Drop it like it's hot! Drop it like it's hot!" Then, "Bust a move! Bust a move!"

To make a long story short, Sam has gone gangsta. He walks the walk and talks the rap. "Wassup?" he'll ask, when he hasn't seen me for all of five minutes. Or he'll tell me he's feeling "all eaten up" when he's not quite himself. He introduces his caregivers as his "homies." Sometimes, he'll go back and forth between rap talk and weather talk, as though he's engaging in parallel conversations: a playa with an obsessive-compulsive interest in meteorology.

That's Sam. Now, let me tell you my story. Recently, Sam's social club, which caters to young adults with various disabilities, sponsored a special outing, a first-ever Boys' Night Out. Where does our fearless outing leader, Tim, decide to take us? To Hooters, of course. And not just any Hooters, but the fancy marina-style Hooters on the Ohio River in downtown Cincinnati.

Everyone arrives early, ready to party. Sam and the other members of his club walk across the wooden ramp one at a time, accompanied by a few of the fathers who serve as helpers, including me. We don't have to worry about fitting in at Hooter's. None of the other customers even notices us. Not the group of Japanese businessmen, not the two grungers wearing heavy metal T-shirts, not the single guy pretending to be reading a newspaper, and certainly not the old geezers sitting at the bar nursing their beers. They're much too busy ogling the Hooters girls to care about a few extraordinary young men limping and shuffling across the wooden floor. The girls are wearing their standard-issue tight shorts and tighter orange tops. The classy look.

"Man, this beats last month's outing," says one of our troops when he spots his first Hooters babe.

"I take care of my guys," says leader Tim, a stocky young man with shoulder-length brown hair. Tim plays in a rock band and appears absolutely unflappable. Nothing ruffles Tim's feathers as he supervises his group: John jumping up and down at the table; Eric scribbling in his notebook left to right, then top to bottom; and Sam asking repeatedly about tornadoes. Just another night out for City Club. Our version of "normal."

Unable to attain Tim's Zen-like state of unflappability, I keep worrying that one of our charges will reach out and grab a handful of Hooters flesh. Ironically, our guys are less distracted by Hooters babes than the other customers. Mostly, we want spicy chicken wings, platters of fries, and a round of drinks, thank you very much. Sure, we enjoy the sexy costumes, but the girls represent only one item on our party platter and definitely not the main course. We're here to party, not to ogle. We don't get out all that much. As you can probably guess, our social calendars aren't very full. But when we do go out on the town, watch out. Let the good times roll!

And for not ogling, the Hooters girls love us. Sure, we're a little weird, but at least we're not sexist pigs. No boorish behavior coming from our table. Just John, the youngest of our group, who is largely nonverbal, bouncing in his seat saying "Hi!" over and over again until it becomes a kind of mantra. So the girls hover around us two and three at a time. They can't resist our charm, like a burst of orange butterflies fluttering around our flowers. And who can blame them? How often does a group of young, distinctive, well-behaved gentlemen appear among Hooters usual clientele?

We're about to order when Eric, a young man about Sam's age, turns to his server and asks, "Do you have a death ray in your mind?"

"Ha ha ha," everyone laughs. Good one, Eric. Our server, a blond bombshell, blushes ever so slightly. She's been asked worse, no doubt.

"No, I don't," she says playfully. "But I have an order pad in my hand, and I can take your order if you're ready."

Eric likes that. You bet. Everyone tries to order at the same time, so that our server has to raise her hand high, like an umpire calling time out. "One at a time, boys."

When it's Sam's turn, he asks, "Wassup? Hey, which do you like better, rap or hip hop?"

"You know, I'm not sure I know the difference," she says. "Can you explain the difference?"

But Sam's already on to the next topic. "Have you ever seen a tornado? Do you remember the Blue Ash tornado on April ninth, 1999? Have the sirens ever gone off here?"

"Whoa," our server says. "You must like weather."

"And fire alarms," Sam adds. He reaches out and touches her arm lightly, then thinks twice about it and snaps his hand back. "Sorry," he says, and means it.

Sam turns to me. "Was I appropriate?"

"Well, don't worry about it. You shouldn't touch, but . . ." I don't know how to finish my sentence.

Later, when we've pretty much finished eating, most of us bearing the telltale signs of catsup and barbecue sauce, the servers take turns coming over to visit.

Then Andrew, our oldest, heads for the gift counter. Someone jokes that he wants to buy a Hooters outfit for his mom. Yeah, right, wouldn't she love that? But when he returns it's with a Hooters T-shirt for himself. We all agree that Andrew will make one handsome dude in his new Hooters T-shirt. Always a ham, Andrew pulls the T-shirt over his head, eyeglasses and all, so we can all see how good he looks. He straightens his glasses and mugs for us and the ladies.

Meanwhile, Sam has cornered another server. "What about the Xenia tornado of 1974? That's famous, you know. The biggest outbreak of tornadoes in recorded history."

"Really?"

"Yeah, I have a book on that one. Do you like fire alarms?"

When we leave, it's with a sense of satisfaction, with the knowledge that we made new friends and interacted with everyone, including the Hooters girls, and that we partied to the max and left quite an impression. We have the T-shirts and catsup stains to prove it. Someone wants to know when and where Tim's rock band will be playing, so that we can continue the party, whenever. Let's do Hooters again. Why not? Hooters rules!

Sam and I are the last to leave. He's made it this far without a serious gaff. But suddenly he reaches out and takes our server's hand and looks deeply into her eyes. "If you were president, you'd be Baberaham Lincoln," he says, repeating a line from the movie *Wayne's World*.

She laughs. "Thank you—I think!"

I breathe a sigh of relief. He could have repeated his favorite line from *Austin Powers: Goldmember*— the one about shagging!

"Did I blow my cover?" he asks on our way out the door, a big grin on his face.

I laugh. "No, we did well."

At that Sam says, "Bust a move!" and does a hip hop dance shuffle on the deck. Then he heads for the ramp that will take him to shore, with me following along behind.

James C. Wilson

The Weird Kid

When our son was diagnosed with PDD-NOS at age four, my husband and I went through the usual rollercoaster of emotions—denial, anger, confusion, and bitterness. Then we began the learning process, doing all the research we could, finding experts, looking into alternative therapies, and just generally running in circles. Once the dust settled, we accepted our son's disorder and began working with the school and other professionals to try to help him succeed.

At age five, our son loved cars and cartoons on TV. He could recite an entire episode of *Arthur*, with perfect inflection, but he couldn't construct a correct sentence of his own from an original thought. He would sometimes blurt out a comment that had nothing to do with the topic at hand. He would repeat the same statement three or four times, seemingly trying to get it right.

He attended a special-needs preschool for a few months after the diagnosis, and then we prepared him to go to public kindergarten, with speech and occupational therapy and other support. It seemed we had all our academic ducks in a row.

But one day, just before he started kindergarten, a thought hit me like a ton of bricks: I was the mother of The Weird Kid. You know The Weird Kid—there was probably one in your class. There was certainly one in your school. Everyone knew who The Weird Kid was. He or she sat alone at lunch, walked the perimeter of the schoolyard alone at recess, and was chosen last for every team. No one wanted to be The Weird Kid's partner for the science project. A new rumor circulated every year: The Weird Kid fried ants under a magnifying glass. The Weird Kid got lost walking home from school. Well, now The Weird Kid was my kid.

When he went off to kindergarten on the bus, my heart was in my throat. He'll be teased mercilessly, I thought. He'll come home every day in tears. So every day, I waited for the bus to drop him off. Every day, he bounced off the bus in good spirits. He had a friend in school who lived down the street and rode the same bus.

When first grade arrived, and they were in school all day, he and his friend ate lunch together and played at recess together. *Okay*, I thought. *This* is great—he has a friend. At least this way, when the teasing starts, he won't be alone. And I kept waiting for his torment to start.

One day when he was in second grade, another kid who lives nearby rode past our house on his bike. Our son was outside and waved to him, and the most miraculous thing happened: The kid stopped, turned his bike around, and rode up our driveway. He stayed for a couple of hours and then said he needed to go home for dinner. I fought the urge to call his mother to see if he could stay another month or two.

In fourth grade, our son decided he wanted to play baseball. Although he was old enough for regular baseball, I signed him up for T-ball, because it was his first time, and I thought he'd have better luck hitting a stationary ball than a moving one. This meant that he'd be on a team with kids a year or two younger than he. *These kids don't know him as well,* I thought, *so there's going to be trouble.*

It turns out that they use the tee in T-ball for only about a week. After that, the coach pitches to the kids. And they keep pitching until the child makes contact with the ball. One day, my son was up at bat. Both he and the coach seemed to be having a bad day. The coach pitched him about two dozen balls, and my son didn't come close to hitting one of them. Then the coach accidentally hit him with a pitch. Then there were six or eight more strikes.

Then he was hit with another pitch and started to cry. The assistant coach asked him if he wanted to sit down, but he said no. Watching helplessly from the sidelines, I thought, *This is it. He's really going to be teased for this.*

After about forty pitches, he finally connected with the ball. Both benches of kids jumped to their feet, yelling, screaming, and clapping. Six or eight of his teammates ran to first base to high-five him when he arrived there. I wasn't sure if they were cheering so much because he got a hit or because his tedious at-bat was finally over, but I realized it really didn't matter. All those kids, even those who didn't know him well, rallied around and cheered him on.

Still, I paid very close attention to the conversations at birthday parties and other events, sure that I would hear whispering or even outright ridicule. I never did. In fact, I once heard one boy, considered by many to be a tough customer, come to my son's defense when another child made a slightly snide remark. All the kids come to his birthday parties, and they all have a great time.

Our son is in seventh grade now, and a core group of kids have been with him all through school. Some of these kids are friends, some are acquaintances, but all of them treat him with respect. I have to give a lot of credit to their parents, who clearly have taught their children to respect others' differences and not to tease, as well as to their teachers. I once commented to one of my son's teachers that I was impressed with how the other kids treat him. He matter-of-factly replied, "We don't ask the kids to respect one another—we require it."

This requirement for respect is obviously more than lip service, though. He's simply one of them, despite his obvious differences. They accept that he repeats things, just as they know that if they have a question about cars, he'll know the answer. They sometimes call him for the homework assignment or ask him to bring their work home if they're absent, just as they would with any neuro-typical classmate.

I still cannot help eavesdropping on conversations among his peers, but I have yet to hear anyone mock him. In my paranoid mother's mind, I sometimes think they're just being polite because I'm around. But he's never complained either. So I have to believe that—whether it's because of parents who teach acceptance, or teachers who won't tolerate intolerance, or kids with naturally open minds and kind hearts, or all of the above—The Weird Kid is no more.

Karen Doyle

Confessions of a Mortal Mom

We're at the lake on a sweltering July day. After hauling our equipment through sand and slathering sunscreen over the kids, I pause to survey the surroundings. Immediately, I spot a toad hopping over sand and shells, about three feet away. Without thinking, I holler, "Hey Ethan—quick! Look what I found." Ethan, in the water, doesn't hear me. I should just drop it; let the poor innocent toad hop on out of our lives, free. Instead, I cup my hands over my mouth and yell louder, "Ethan—come look. Hurry!"

A bit put out, like I'm interrupting a business meeting, my nine-year-old son tears himself away from two new pals to saunter over and see what inconsequential information his mother has for him. At first, he doesn't see the toad. "What is it?"

"Look. Right there."

His gaze follows my pointing index finger and sees the prize. With a cat's agility, he pounces. The toad barely has time to struggle. In a blink, Ethan is holding it, examining it. His eyes narrow, and the seven freckles on his nose disappear in wrinkles of concentration. His brown hair, still dry, has been cut in a faux Mohawk.

"Know what, Mom? This is a spade-foot toad."

"Really?" I'm sure he's right. He's definitely an expert on reptiles and amphibians.

"Can I keep it?"

"We'll see."

Watching him show off his toad, I resist the urge to breathe a sigh of relief. My mind wanders back to another summer day seven years ago, the day Ethan scored a forty-two on the Childhood Autism Rating Scale (CARS), which meant he had moderate to severe autism.

Sarah, the speech pathologist at Children's Hospital, greeted Ethan, my husband, Richard, and me in the lobby. Ethan, two and a half, ignored her and headed for the drinking fountain. He peered intently inside the vent, trying to see the motor. I peeled him off, and he flailed his limbs and yelled unintelligible words in protest.

In the testing room, he spotted a cup of marbles. Fascinated, he played exclusively with them, as if nothing else existed. Finally, Sarah took away the cup and put the marbles outside the door. Still, my darling toddler, dressed in black jeans, a polo shirt, and cowboy boots, refused to submit to the formal testing procedure. He preferred kicking and screaming on the floor, utterly ignoring the dolls, play stove, and train set.

Midway through the evaluation, as I chewed my fingernails while I watched Ethan stack and restack blocks, I knew what was coming. I'd already devoured three books on autism and was kicking myself for not having gotten the diagnosis a year earlier. Richard, however, looked like Jack Bauer after a harrowing episode of *24*.

Autism became my archenemy at that point, and I vowed to join the breed of mothers it seems to produce: faster than a speeding bullet, more powerful than a locomotive—mothers who have not only cured their children but also achieved PhDs, written books, and become international public speakers on the side. I donned my Spandex suit and red cape and took off on my quest to turn my Pinocchio into a real boy.

I heard about an ABA (Applied Behavioral Analysis) program and found a psychologist willing to work with us. I scheduled an introductory workshop and recruited a staff of college student tutors to work with Ethan. We couldn't afford the $1,100 workshop, but I didn't care. I made some calls, and the local ARC generously donated the entire amount.

The workshop took place one day after Ethan's third birthday. He had no words in his vocabulary, except perhaps "binky" (for his pacifier), which he was too old to be asking for anyway. The second day of the workshop, for the first time in his life, he repeated a couplet, the command, "Do this." Through my tears, I became a devotee of Dr. Ivar Lovaas.

I spent the next two years juggling schedules, working with Ethan myself, alienating my husband and daughter, tracking down funding sources, cutting out ten different shapes in eleven different colors and five different sizes, buying tons of educational toys and reward candy, keeping the house somewhat clean for the daily parade of college students, and diligently recording the antecedent, behavior, and consequence for each of Ethan's many tantrums. It exhausted me, but I clenched my teeth and dug in harder.

Back then, if someone had asked me how having a child with autism impacted my life, I would have said it was about learning to persevere in the face of adversity. In the end, I would defeat the enemy, Ethan would graduate from Harvard with distinction, and this situation would yield our finest hour. Failure was not an option.

Today, soaking up sun at the beach, I scoff at that notion. Bringing me back to the present, Ethan and the other kids come to shore in search of grapes and juice pouches. Ethan still has the toad; he has decided to name it "Africa Five."

"I'm not sure they let kids keep toads." I tear the plastic off a straw and jab it into the foil pouch. The negotiations have begun.

"But, Mom, look at him. He's injured. He needs someone to take care of him."

I look at Africa Five. Ethan's right: only three legs. "We'll see. I'll have to check with the park rangers." A scheme forms in my mind. I'll get out of this by passing the buck. It'll be the park rangers who say no, not me.

"Come on, Mom, please."

"I don't know. We don't even have an aquarium."

"I can put him in one of those plastic tubs."

"Then what'll we do with the toys?"

He shrugs. "Put them in a regular box."

Oh, sure, that will look classy in the family room. "I'll think about it."

I hate saying no to Ethan. While he's outgrown the screaming, kicking, pinching, head-banging, body-slamming, biting tantrums, he still talks trash. He's still a master at pushing my buttons, so (wimp though I may be) I try very hard to avoid locking horns. The kids finish eating, drop their towels, and return to splashing and sand piles.

I observe Ethan surrounded by kids, showing off his toad, letting them have a turn holding it—Mr.

Congeniality. If I didn't know him, I'd probably have no idea he has autism. When it comes to things that interest him, he can be a walking encyclopedia. He uses big words and can hold his own in many technical or philosophical discussions. Who would know he can barely read?

A few minutes later, he returns. "Guess what, Mom? They said I can keep it."

"Who?"

"Those police officers." My gaze follows his finger to three park rangers seated at a picnic table.

"Oh." Darn. Looks like he just won the negotiation. I consider the logistics involved with keeping yet another toad until my thoughts mosey back several years, to the end of Ethan's behavioral program . . . and the demise of my Super Mom dream.

The tantrums were the main antagonists. We used a process called "extinction and redirection", and they were supposed to stop but didn't. Instead, they intensified. I blamed the college students. They blamed me. The psychologist sided with them, and things got ugly. I lost confidence in my parenting ability. It was up to me to cure this kid, but I couldn't.

I tried some alternative treatments. Richard and I gave Ethan two infusions of the acclaimed miracle drug, Secretin. Then we put him on a gluten-free, casein-free diet. I learned to make cookies and fake-cheese pizza with rice flour and potato-based dry milk. I lived at Vitamin Cottage and read nutrition encyclopedias for entertainment.

Everything cost money, scarce at our house. Still, I dove in with my blinders on. The ABA program, along with toys, special diet food, and miscellaneous items, cost an extra $2,500 every month. We took out a second mortgage and then refinanced again. Suddenly, our home equity was gone, but it was worth it, wasn't it? Wouldn't it all be justified in the end? After all, I had heard someone (another Super Mom) argue that if you had a kid with a brain tumor, you'd do everything in your power to help. Why not do everything possible, then, to help your kid overcome autism?

The difference, in my humble opinion, is that no one expects the mom to cure the child's brain tumor. In the autism world, however, there exists a subtle pressure. I got the feeling that if I was reasonably intelligent, curing Ethan was within my grasp. I should be able to do this.

The ABA program ended on a Saturday morning. Following a tantrum incident, the psychologist called and said she could no longer work with us. That was it—poof!—the end. All that work and money down the drain. I, Super Mom wanna-be, handled the stress by opening the refrigerator and feeding my frustration. I also avoided Ethan's "therapy room" for a month. So much for failure not being an option.

Fortunately, Ethan was saved by the local pre-school, a true miracle—something that even Super Mom couldn't have arranged. The teachers genu-inely loved Ethan. They recognized his potential and encouraged his natural curiosity. They treated him with dignity and respect. And then, once again miraculously, the tantrums stopped.

At a conference, the preschool director said she believed everyone needs an Ethan in their lives. Why? "Because he's so literal. He sees the world from a different angle, one worth considering. He makes us think." She claimed it was easy for adults to be drawn to Ethan, at times even at the expense of other kids, because he had such a novel perspective on things. She said he was a "delight to be around."

Nonetheless, I continued my slide into the Pit of Depression. I ate so much that I popped the seams right out of my Spandex suit and had to throw it away. Who cared? There was nothing left to do but sit in front of the TV all day eating bon-bons and watching *Oprah*. Then it happened, another miracle. During our two-month free cable period, I stumbled upon the movie, Rudy.

It was the true story of Daniel Ruteger, a little guy who dreamed of playing football for Notre Dame. Everyone told him he couldn't do it, but after lots of trying and lots of failing, he finally got his fifteen min-utes. In one scene, Rudy, discouraged, went to church and talked to a priest. At one point the priest said, "In my thirty-five years of religious studies, I've come to believe in two incontrovertible facts. One, there is a God. And two, I'm not him." It set me free.

When it comes to autism and Super Moms, I can't count myself among them. But truth be told, it doesn't matter. I have a great God and a great kid, and that's enough. Besides, the jury's still out. Ethan may graduate from Harvard with distinction . . . or may not. Either way, it doesn't matter; I love him and couldn't be prouder of him just the way he is. My job is to help him find his strengths and reach his potential, not to control the outcome. The outcome is not in my hands.

At the lake, we pack up Africa Five in a cardboard box full of wet sand. So, the toad is missing a leg—big deal. Even if people notice, it doesn't matter; Ethan loves it and couldn't be prouder. On the way out, he stops to thank the park rangers, and for a few minutes, they chat like old friends. I smile. The preschool director was right. He's a delight to be around. As for me, I'm a mere mortal, but that doesn't make me a failure. I am blessed.

Sonja Predovich

Getting Along

Mike is talking to himself again. I hear his sing-song voice tell about a bad man hiding things in a sandbox each time I walk past the bathroom door. His words blur together, much as they have since he finally began to talk at the age of five. Seventeen now, he is still talking nonsense.

Mike is my nephew, a tall, thin boy with a sharp nose and wire glasses that make him look like the actor who plays Harry Potter in the movies. I once made the mistake of mentioning this.

"I hate that guy!" he yelled, and slapped his head several times before running to hide in his room.

While Mike takes a bath, I carry firewood from the porch and stack it by the wood-burning stove. Our weekend in the family's mountain cabin will be an experiment for us, to see how we get along. His father, my brother, Pete, died eight months ago. His mother is too ill to take care of him.

As I line up rows of logs, I wonder how, or even whether, Mike regards his orphaned future. He seldom talks seriously and seems interested only in taking apart small electronic devices, like clocks and cell phones. He has Asperger's syndrome.

He was three when we first met. As soon as I got out of the car in front of Pete's new house, skinny little Mike, dressed only in underpants, climbed into my arms and stayed there for the entire two hours of my visit. While Pete narrated a tour, Mike steered me through the rooms by leaning, pointing, and crooning vowel sounds. When, at last, I put him down to say goodbye, his blue eyes stared past me.

He started school two years late and took special classes. Now he is a high school junior. His only friends are a succession of much younger boys who briefly tolerate his repetitive habits and immature outbursts.

Those outbursts can hurt. A few years ago, I played my cello for him and other friends and family.

"That sounds really bad," Mike said after a few minutes. He got up and left the room. Even now, my face heats up when I recall the awkward, ensuing silence.

The clink of metal on metal brings me back to the cabin. Mike has finished his bath, dressed himself in a dragon T-shirt and too-short pants, and started tinkering with gadgets on the oak dining table. With precision and delicacy, using tweezers and a screw-driver, he is opening my cell phone to disconnect and then reconnect its twisted wires, to inspect its inner workings. He can fix almost anything.

I invite him to go on a hike, but he calls the mountains "boring" and the beavers "retarded." That's fine with me. I relish my time alone in these meadows and aspen groves. As the sun falls behind the peaks, turning the fields from yellow to blue-green, I walk up one stream and down the other. A month ago, there were eleven beaver dams, and now there are twenty-five. Mike won't care. When I return to the cabin, I find that he has climbed the ladder to the loft, posted a Keep Out sign, and fallen asleep.

At dinner, though, we talk. He asks me riddles I can't answer and makes up harmless lies.

"I like to mess with you," he says frankly. With a sideways glance, he points and yells, "Watch out for the bear!" before grabbing the last cookie.

I discover that I like his sly brand of teasing. When we laugh together, I feel waves of affection for this odd boy.

Surprising me again, he mutters "thank you" for dinner and agrees, with only a little arm-twisting, to do the dishes. This gives me time to slip over to the guest cabin and practice my cello. I ask him if he minds, but he doesn't answer. He's standing at the sink, intently watching water flow out of the faucet and soap bubbles rise in the basin.

I'm working on a new piece, having a devil of a time with it. The frustration plagues me, as do the pine boughs that scratch my cheek in the dark and the damp grasses that sting my legs as I feel my way down the hill, across the foot bridge, and up the rock steps to the cabin. In particular, I'm trying to learn to bounce the bow so it will play quick, short notes evenly, in rhythm. The move is called "down-bow spiccato."

As I sit in the log cabin with the cello between my knees, trying to bounce the bow, Mike walks in without knocking.

"Can I listen?" he asks.

"Sure," I say, showing more welcome than I feel.

He sits on the couch and stares at me coolly, his gaze impenetrable. I feel a rush of stage fright. *This is ridiculous,* I tell myself. *I can tolerate the presence of this young critic. He knows nothing about the cello, and I've been playing it all my life. Besides, I'm well-adjusted, and he isn't. He's the one with a diagnosis. To heck with it.* I launch into a folk melody section I know well.

"That's cool," says Mike.

He settles more comfortably into the couch. Emboldened, I turn a few pages to find the tough place in the third movement, the one I'm working on.

"Okay," I say apologetically, "I don't know this yet. There's a chord, and then there's this hard section with all these short notes in spiccato . . ."

His steady stare stops my chatter. He says nothing.

I have to play four notes in one motion, drawing the bow from left to right so it bounces evenly the whole way. It should sound effortless, but the bow feels clumsy in my hand. The notes blurt out, all different sizes and shapes.

Mike looks me in the eye. "I like this music."

I appraise him. He is not messing with me.

"But I can't figure out this bowing," I confide. "My teacher tells me what to do and I try, but it doesn't work." He turns on the couch, and I turn on the wooden chair so that we face each other. "What I want," I say, "is four even notes in one bow, like this." I attempt to show him what I can't do.

"Can I try?" he asks.

We switch places. Mike sits in the hard chair, and with a little trepidation, I position the cello close to his body, balanced on its endpin, so it rests against his chest. Then I show him how to hold the bow. He ignores me and holds it his own way.

"So you want it to bounce four times?" he asks, moving the bow so it bounces four times.

"How did you do that?" I'm stunned. He's messing with me in a big way now.

He repeats the stroke again and again, watching objectively. "See my muscles?" Mike flexes his right arm so the tendons of his hand and forearm pop into relief. "I'm meatless, so you can see my gross muscles. You know I'm really gross, don't you, Kim?" he says with a wry smile. He wiggles his fingers and flexes his wrist to animate the show in his forearm.

I study his muscles with envy. "Do it again," I say.

Mike does it again. He bounces the bow from frog to tip, articulating the notes clearly along the way. I watch; he obliges.

"You try," he says at last, turning the cello on its pin and standing to give me the chair.

I take my cello and my bow, the ones I have played for twenty years, and humbly try to copy his motions. The bow bounces high for two notes and then flounders. On my next try, it springs so far out of control that I get seven notes instead of four.

With quiet concentration, Mike studies my arm, the bow, and the cello. "What you have to do," he says, "is turn the bow away from you, so more hair is on the string. The other thing is to hold the bow from here," he says, pointing to the tendon of his right arm, "so this gross part helps. If your muscle is puny, you could make it stronger by turning screws with a screwdriver. You could just practice. You wouldn't have to make something, if you just had an old board."

Dumbfounded, I let his words sink in. Mike is telling me, in substance, exactly what I heard from my teacher, a cellist in the Chicago Symphony Orchestra.

But that isn't what amazes me most. I knew about Mike's talent for discerning how things work. The surprise is that not once, not that day nor any day since, has Mike messed with me about the cello lesson. He has not bragged or put me down. This strange boy, who has proven on one test after another that he can't understand most of what goes on between people, can be a kind and patient teacher. When he has something real to give, he is generous.

Mike has a good home now; he went to live with his warm and welcoming aunt and uncle a few weeks later. They are teaching him good manners and nurturing the empathy that began to emerge that day in the cabin. He and I meet for weekends in Colorado when we can. He still puts up the Keep Out sign, and I still can't bounce the bow, but we're both learning.

Katherine Millett

Brothers

The light reflecting off the bath water swirled up around my sons' blond heads and tinged their skin pink. My younger son, Jonny, age three, imitated his five-year-old brother, Jefferson, by slamming his fist down into the bubbles. I stifled my protests as I watched them play, the bath water flying in abandon as the two boys pealed with laughter. I knew some of my friends, also mothers of young boys, would probably blanch at my cavalier behavior, but I just sat quietly, occasionally wiping away an errant drop from the rhythmic slap-fest going on before me. My smile was so big my cheeks hurt; my heart was filled with awe and gratitude.

Just nine months earlier, bath time had been quite a different scene: very loud on one end of the shared tub, deathly quiet on the other. Jefferson's booming voice would echo off the blue and white checkered bath tiles as he pleaded with his little brother to play with him or to simply take notice of him.

"Watch me, Jonny! Look at me!" he would yell, while doing something silly like putting a toy on his head or driving a truck deep into the bubbles. But Jonny was oblivious to the sounds around him, his bright blue eyes focused intently on the water poured from a cup into his outstretched fingers, ignoring his brother's cries, just inches away . . . and breaking my heart.

"Why won't he look at me?" Jefferson asked, his brow furrowed in a way much too old for a five-year-old.

"Jonny just sees the world differently," I said, searching for an explanation about autism that a young child might understand, while realizing I could barely understand it myself. "He's learning how to talk, but he might not know what 'me' means, you know? For instance, sometimes I'm 'me,' right? And sometimes you're 'me.'"

Jefferson nodded slowly, wiping a tiny drop of water from his nose, his soft brown eyes reflecting my own burning question: "Would Jonny ever learn to play with his big brother?"

The vice cinched tighter on my heart as I continued. "It gets confusing for Jonny. So how about, since he knows your name, you say, 'Look at Jeff,' instead of 'Look at me.' Maybe that will work."

Each night after that conversation as I drew the bath, I silently wished for a breakthrough with Jonny—anything to give me a glimmer of hope. I would stare at the gleaming white porcelain, willing it to work its magic, as if the tub surface could affect neurotransmission.

Several nights passed with no change. Jonny continued to passively lift cups of water to eye level and watch the water rain down, continually repeating the process. Jefferson's frustration mounted along with the decibel level of his voice.

On the fourth night after our conversation, however, after Jefferson once again began his new litany of chants—"Look at Jeff, Jonny! Look at Jeff!"—an amazing thing happened: Jonny looked. I could still hear faint echoes of his commands reverberating off the bathroom walls as Jefferson and I screamed with delight, high-fiving each other and Jonny, trying to show him how much his interaction meant to us.

It was the first of many milestones to follow.

As the months went by, Jonny's teachers worked hard to help him link faces with names, and he started requesting interactive play with his older brother, saying, "Get Jeff," or "Chase Jeff." He was making exciting progress at his early intervention school, adding new words to his vocabulary and using the Picture Exchange Communication System (PECS) to learn sentence structure and build upon his communication skills. Although people gave my husband and me credit for our work at home with Jonny, it was largely Jefferson who was becoming his at-home therapist.

After some gentle guidance from me, Jefferson quickly learned how to help Jonny find his binder filled with pictures that he used to communicate his desires. He also found new ways to get through to Jonny. He made sure to make eye contact, stooping so he was face-to-face when he talked to his little brother, while being careful not to use pronouns and to speak in very simple sentences.

He rewarded Jonny for any interaction, screaming out, "Good looking, Jonny!" if the small boy gave him eye contact. Or he would say "good talking" or "good job" for any small achievement. Once aloof and disconnected, Jonny now hugged his big brother tightly while softly saying in Jefferson's ear, "Oh, that's nice."

Jefferson beamed with every hug.

The house began to fill with laughter as Jefferson found new ways to entertain his little brother, often by eliciting strange bodily noises from his mouth. Jonny started to mimic Jefferson's actions more often—jumping into a bean bag chair while saying a special word or small phrase, or running on the grass and falling over in giggles just like his big brother. He also became Jefferson's 3-foot-tall echo.

Jefferson would call out to me, "Mom! I'm hungry!" Then moments later, I would hear Jonny's tiny voice: "Mom! I'm hungry!" He was learning through imitation; something most kids do at infancy, but with autism it comes much later, if at all. Jefferson prompted Jonny to follow his lead, and I could tell he took pride in each of Jonny's achievements.

He knew he was becoming the teacher.

Not only was his work with Jonny helping his little brother interact with the world, it was changing who Jefferson was and how he interacted with the world outside our home as well. He would applaud other children's successes at the playground, even complimenting older kids' abilities, craning his neck to look up at the older child and saying, "You do the monkey bars really well," or telling a small child, "Good climbing," when they reached the top of a rope ladder.

Recently, some of Jefferson's kindergarten classmates gathered in a quiet, curious semi-circle around Jonny.

"Why doesn't he talk?" one boy asked.

I fought the urge to jump in with an explanation, desperately wanting to defend Jonny without making him seem odd. Instead, having not mastered explaining autism to the general population, let alone to a group of five-year-olds, I decided to sit back and let Jefferson explain it in his words, his way.

Jefferson looked over at his little brother, analyzing the little blond boy sitting mute in his stroller, his squinting gaze dropping from the children surrounding him to his tiny hands folded in his lap. All Jefferson said was, "He talks, just not here."

The simple, insightful response seemed to work. The other kids seemed satisfied with that, and let it go.

When my husband, Dan, and I first talked about having a second child, the comment, "Jefferson will have a playmate," was a large part of our decision. But after Jonny's diagnosis and as we watched our small toddler slowly disengage from the world, I wondered if Jefferson would be faced with a lifelong burden rather than a lifelong companion.

I never contemplated the idea that Jonny's diagnosis might be the best thing to ever happen to our older son. But as the therapy progressed for Jonny and Jefferson continued to participate in the process, I could see changes in both boys. And I began to see their interaction in a new way: What if every challenge we are faced with includes a lesson we need to learn to have a better life? What if the choices we make regarding life's difficulties shapes us into the person we will need to be in order to face even tougher challenges ahead?

I could resign myself to believe that Jonny's affliction with autism was just a random act of biology, but where is the magic in that?

I know that as Jefferson gets older, he will have to explain Jonny's autism to his friends and classmates and that it will become more difficult as peer pressure builds. He will have to come to grips with his brother's unique behaviors and decide that it is okay to be different. It will be one of many important choices Jefferson will be faced with, and I only hope I can gently direct him down the right paths.

I feel confident he will make the right decisions, and I take comfort in one truth: Whatever the future holds, both Jefferson and Jonny are going to be better people because they are brothers.

Jennifer Finn Wake

The Singing Blues

My parents met in a mandolin orchestra. From the time I was little, I heard them play beautiful duets together, with melody lines passing playfully back and forth between the two instruments. Our home was always full of music. I took piano lessons, dabbled in the viola, and played the trombone in my high school band. I also sang in choirs from the age of ten. So when I became a mother, singing to my baby came as naturally to me as nursing him or constantly sniffing and kissing his sweet head.

Every day and night, I would sing to Zachary: lullabies, nursery rhymes, oldies that my mother had sung to me. When he was an infant, we would snuggle into a favorite upholstered chair and I would serenade my baby boy as I cradled him in my arms. I remember the way he would gaze up deeply into my eyes and how his tiny hand felt against my skin. It was rapturous to enfold him and croon away. Sometimes we even danced. He loved all the tunes, and before he could talk he would coo along and attempt to phonetically fill in a word at the end of a phrase, which I would pretend to have forgotten. Then, suddenly, at about age three, he stopped liking it. Each time I would start to sing, Zachary would cry. It was mostly the lullabies and softer tunes that set him off. He'd wail loudly and atonally. I stopped singing.

Every few months I'd try again—but there was no way. Within a few notes, Zach's mournful wails would stop my singing. Never before had I made a listener cry (that I know of). Some days, it felt like the worst rejection I had ever known, as though it were not the music he was pushing away, but me. His reaction stung—like a slap.

What we didn't know when he was an infant but soon learned was that Zach has a form of autism. Although he is quite high-functioning, he has many challenges. One of the physical disorders with which my son copes courageously is hypersensitivity. This means he hears, sees, feels, smells, and tastes things more intensely than most other people do. So, for example, when a neighbor down the street would mow the lawn, Zach would pace frantically around the house with his forearms over his ears until the noise stopped. Although he has learned to manage most of the auditory stuff, Zach still struggles with certain sounds. And he still can't endure the sight or feel of wet-looking or creamy foods, preferring those with dry surfaces. Just looking at cream cheese, peanut butter, or cake batter can trigger a gag reflex. When he was about a year old and starting to eat solid foods, we wanted to encourage self-feeding. I discovered that if I wrapped tiny pieces of meat and vegetables in bread and left them on his highchair tray, he'd pick them up and devour them. Otherwise, he refused to touch food—no matter how hungry he was.

Though I rationalized that his acute reaction to my singing was the result of his hypersensitivity, sometimes it still hurt my feelings. I soothed my pain by telling myself that it was simply the sound that hurt his ears.

As the years passed, Zachary developed a love for popular music and begged me to tune in the rock 'n roll stations on the radio whenever we were in the car. This music didn't seem to bother him at all. Au contraire! The louder the better. He also invented complex rhythms and enjoyed lying on his back in the bathtub with his ears just under the surface of the water, repeating them at peak volume, over and over. "Ta-ka ta-ka ta, ta-ka ta, ta, ta!"

So why did Mom's singing make him cry? I stoically mourned the loss of my pleasurable pastime and moved on, but I still tried, every once in a while, hoping against hope that it had been "a phase."

At bedtime I'd say, "Zachary, why don't you choose a song for us to sing." He'd select a rollicking rendition of "Old MacDonald Had a Farm" or a jazzy version of "The Itsy-Bitsy Spider," but never the exquisite "The Lion Sleeps Tonight," or heaven forbid, "Hush Little Baby."

Once a year or so, I'd ask him why he cried when I sang. His answer was always the same: "I don't know."

Then, a few years ago on the eve of Valentine's Day, I was putting seven-year-old Zach to bed, talking about the next day at school, when his class was having a party and the kids would be exchanging cards. He was very excited about it.

"Mom, you know, I really like Sandra, but I also like Bettina," he said.

"It's okay to like a lot of different people, sweetheart."

"But, Mom, I want you to be my real Valentine."

I was very moved. I said, "Zach, you will always be my Valentine." Then I spontaneously started to sing one of my favorite old standards: "My funny valentine, sweet comic valentine. . . ." I never made it to the second line. Zach buried his face in his pillow and started to cry. Of course, I stopped singing immediately and felt terrible. After a moment, he stopped crying. I dried his tears and held him in my arms, rocking him gently.

Then I said, "Zachary, I want you to take as much time as you need and try to use your words to tell me why you cry when I sing to you."

We stayed quiet for a very long time—maybe two full minutes. Finally, he said, "Mom, it's too beautiful."

Lorri Benedik

Word Games

Don't you just love it when your kid learns a new word? Kids like mine seem to have an affinity for certain aspects of language. Sounds, syllables, rhythm, rhyme. Do you know how many words rhyme with, for example, "turd"? Of course, as parents of any type kid can tell you, the less appropriate the word, the more appeal it holds. The difference between my kid and "other" kids is that the other kids know intuitively that one sneaks out behind the barn to share knowledge of and become proficient in the use of such contraband.

Now, it's one thing when my son sits in his bedroom, muttering and giggling to himself: "turd . . . bird . . . word . . . curd . . . heard . . . turdy birdy wordy curdy dirty. . . ." Or takes a word-find puzzle and circles all the "asses" he can find. (Those word-finds are treasure troves of asses let me tell you, and then, of course, there's our favorite word, "assassinate.")

But this kid has trouble differentiating between the privacy of his home and the public arena of, say, the grocery store. Put another way, "inhibition" is neither in his dictionary nor in his neurons.

When he asked, "Mommy, what's a whore?" I told him I needed to think really hard about the meaning of the word. With "most" kids, you can go ahead and tell them what a whore is. They'll file the information in their built-in Inhibit This file, and only spew it forth behind the barn with their pals.

With my kid, that is to say, with an Asperger's kid, you don't want to tell him precisely what a whore is when he's nine; when he's twelve, you're still not so sure he needs to know—especially when money is a prime behavioral motivator, as it is for my kid. I knew exactly what his reaction would be. Even in the middle of a peaceful library, he'd yell, "Wow, cool, you can get money for sex?" (Money he likes; the other he still considers yucky.) "Why wouldn't a woman want to be a whore? I wish I were a woman so I could be a whore and earn money for having sex!"

Nope. Didn't want that to happen. So I needed time to decide how to present the concept in a way that would not be appealing, and I certainly wasn't going to point out that whoredom is gender-blind. Fortunately, at nine he was satisfied to know I'd tell him once "I figured out how to explain it so you'll understand." That was, after all, the plain truth.

Three years passed, during which he researched the joys of Dogdom. "Mom, can you take me for a walk? Here's my leash." "Hello, SPCA? My neighbor's kid's loose again; he barked at me and chased my cats, peed in the rose bushes, and . . . and . . . I'm worried, because this is trash night." I forgot about the "W" word, and so too, I assumed, did my son.

I didn't reckon with rap music.

When a kid at school let him listen in on his Walkman, my son was thrilled to sneak in a few rap songs with prevalent use of the "F" word. The teacher wisely told the other kids in class—who knew to keep their mouths shut or to go the heck out behind the barn—not to let him listen to their music. He'd sit and bob his head, grinning and singing along out loud. Hey, it's a great word, and do you know how many other words rhyme with it? He's especially thrilled with the exotic phenomenon of weaving the "F" word into the middle of another word ("absoef-finlutely!"). Recently, one of his classmates told the teacher that the rap song on his Walkman didn't have any cuss words in it, so she allowed my kid to listen to the song.

On Valentine's Day, he said, "Mom, what's a ho?"

Clonk went my head on the steering wheel.

"Is it true that a ho is somebody who goes out with a lot of people and gets sexy with all of them?"

Clonk. "Yes, honey. And you know that's not a good thing, right?"

"Yeah, you can get AIDS and stuff. But I like the way it sounds. And there's a Pokémon called Ho-oh. Is Ho-oh a ho?" Giggle, giggle. "Ho . . . Ho . . . Ho . . . Ho . . ."

Clonk. "We have to go into the store, now, and you know what that means."

"No inappropriate words."

"Right." I forgot to tell Mr. Literal that "ho" is not particularly appropriate, even though it's not in the same league as the "F" word. I was too busy feeling grateful we're not Hopi and wondering what will happen at Christmas time when he realizes Santa says "Ho-ho-ho." (Clonk, clonk, clonk.) In view of those insights, I decided the Jolly Green Giant section in the frozen foods aisle was to be avoided at all cost.

It being Cupid's special day, our grocery store had a Valentine's Express checkout line. Fortunately, we had a heart-shaped ice cream cake in our cart and so qualified, despite the three cube-shaped gallons of milk. On this day of lovers, the youthful checker, who has bonded with my son in the past over Pokémon, was dressed all in pink. Sparkles decorated her eyes and her cheeks. She looked adorable.

She smiled at my son and, anticipating her weekly pop Pokémon quiz, quickly said, "I remember your Pokémon's name."

My son grinned back at her, held up his stuffed Celebi, as always, and asked, "Are you a ho?"

Clonk. Riiiip. Clonk. Boooiiing! As my head cracked the conveyor belt and my hair was dragged underneath the scanner, I heard her jaw hit the floor and saw her eyes pop out of their sockets.

Once in the safe confines of our car, I explained precisely what a whore is, the negative social implications thereof, why it is insulting to ask the question he had asked, and why he would never again ask a woman—or a man, for that matter—if s/he is a ho or a whore. (One must cover one's favorite word-find puzzle word.)

"Mom?"

"Yes?"

"Is that why you didn't want to tell me what a whore was when I was nine?"

Clonk.

Nan Jacobs

An Exercise in Acceptance

The seat rests directly on the floor—cushion on the bottom, aluminum back, covered with material. This is my first encounter with the floor chair, but it will not be my last. In fact, I will come to associate the floor chair with personal and spiritual growth. Eventually, the mere sight of one of these simple chairs will cause a tingle up my spine in anticipation of an encounter with my higher self.

My husband and I have traveled to this place, in western Massachusetts, hoping to learn how to deal with our own emotions in relation to our three-year-old daughter, recently diagnosed with an autistic spectrum disorder.

We don't want anything to be wrong with our baby, but this diagnosis at least offers an explanation for her volatile behavior: Wailing when she steps outside into the sunlight, "It's too bright! It hurts!" Collapsing on the floor, hands over ears, shrieking in panic over the sound of a sneeze. Tantrums in restaurants in response to noises, smells, the over-stimulation of it all.

When she isn't overwhelmed, she is as sweet as they come . . . a little Jekyll and Hyde. I am astonished how I can go from adoring her to despising her in a split second, my own grown-up Jekyll and Hyde show. This isn't what I signed up for when I conceived her. I'm not cut out for this. So often, I just want to give up. I need help.

Learning about what she's going through on the inside has helped to make sense of her behavior, but this has been going on for a long time, and I am exhausted. Exhausted from the constant judgments from family and strangers. She looks so normal. They just don't get it. "Give me one day with that child, and I'll take care of her problem!" they say. Exhausted from explaining it isn't a discipline issue. Exhausted from wondering if maybe it is.

If she truly has sensory integration dysfunction, we need to face the fact that no magic cure is going to make it go away. We'll do what we can to help her, but we must delve deeply inward and figure out a way to accept her, exactly as she is. This is the reason we are here.

We have broken into groups of two. I am paired with a stranger, and we are sitting across from one another, firmly planted on our floor chairs, about to begin a healing exercise. Our knees are almost touching. My partner is tiny, her short hair in tight blond curls. Her nametag reads "Susan." She looks to be in her mid-forties. She has a blanket wrapped tightly around her. Susan seems frail and more chilled than she should be. She is bird-like, and as she adjusts her wrap, I see one of her "wings" is being held secure in a sling. The exercise is being guided by a moderator, and we are instructed to look into each other's eyes. Susan's eyes are a beautiful blue. This is very uncomfortable. I don't know her. I try not to look away, but my eyes seem to have minds of their own and divert from hers at least a couple of times.

There are about 100 people in the room, fifty pairs. About 100 other parents going through the same things we are, or worse. I glance about and see my husband partnered with a woman wearing a religious head cover. Her too? My heart warms. For her. For him. We are all the same.

The moderator speaks, and I'm back with Susan. We are instructed to think about a situation we are working on and to tell our partner our fears about it. I am speaking first, and I tell Susan about my daughter. About her diagnosis. About her tantrums. About my fear that I am not capable of giving her what she needs. How I lack the patience and the wisdom to be a good mother to her. How I sometimes want to give up. Susan listens and nods, clearly in the moment with me.

Time is up, and the nonspeaking partner is instructed to argue my case back to me and to go for the jugular.

Susan says, "Sounds like your daughter is really a little monster. She must be awful to live with."

"Well, she's not a monster. She has a neurological condition, and she sometimes has a really hard time."

"Still," she says, "Who would want to put up with her fussing all the time? Doesn't sound like you have much of a life at all."

"Well, there is a lot of good that comes with her too. She has a beautiful heart, and she's kind and sweet. She is loving and empathetic and wise beyond her years."

"Still, you don't seem to have the patience or the wisdom to deal with a kid like that. Sounds like she's ruining your life. Why don't you just give up? Put her in an institution someplace, maybe a good boarding school that can handle kids like her, where they can train her to behave."

Silence.

I am well aware this is an exercise, but I am shocked by her candor. My inner lioness jolts upright onto her haunches.

With my eyes, I say, *Look here, you little know-nothing twit of a woman!*

With my voice, I say: "I am the only one on this earth equipped for this job. I know this little girl. I know her heart. No one at any institution is going to be able to give her the one thing she needs the most, which is her mother's love. If anyone is ever going to help her, it is going to be me, and it is going to be through my total loving acceptance of her."

Susan's eyes are locked on my glare. One second . . . two seconds . . . three seconds. A softness comes over her face, followed by a gentle smile. She nods. Three more seconds, and I am sobbing. As it turns out, in my heart of hearts, I really do want this job.

My daughter is five now. We have found many therapies that have helped her, including occupational therapy, auditory integration training, I Can Do It Too gymnastics, and others. Most recently, we started methylated B_{12} injection therapy, which has reduced her anxiety immensely. We would never have found any of these treatments if we hadn't first gotten a handle on our own emotions and begun to accept our daughter for who she is. This has been and continues to be primarily a spiritual journey. For us, it began in Sheffield, Massachusetts, on little aluminum chairs with seats that sat directly on the floor.

Michelle O'Neil

A Child Slips the Bonds of Earth

When my daughter was six years old, she returned to school after the weekend with an oozing red-brown welt on her left wrist. And it was my fault. But she wouldn't tell you that. Since Talia has autism, she couldn't explain how it happened.

It started on a sunny day at a country fall fair. Surrounded by disco music and shrieking roller-coaster riders, we strolled and enjoyed the aroma of candy apples. Together we climbed the rickety metal stairs on the yellow wave slide. Talia, as tiny as a toddler, grinned as she ascended, carefully placing two feet side-by-side on each step. Glancing at the crowds below us, I gripped the rail tightly.

At the top, I spread out the burlap mat and lifted her onto it. For safety, I wanted her to sit between my legs for the ride. But as I struggled to sit on the narrow slide, she started to slip away from me. I reached out and grabbed the back of her T-shirt, pulling her off the protective burlap. Then, both of us careened down the hot slide.

Because Talia didn't cry, I assumed she was fine. But then I noticed her rubbing her wrist. On her descent, the friction of the slide against her flesh had burned her hand. If I hadn't held onto her, she would have sailed down solo, laughing with excitement. Instead, she was in pain.

Other parents struggled with similar issues at the fair. I overheard one conversation between a mother and her daughter as they approached the carousel.

"Do you want Mummy to go with you?" asked the woman.

"No."

"You want to go all by yourself?"

"Yes."

"Then you have to hold on tight to the pole, and you can't keep turning your head to look for Mummy."

This was hardly a typical parent/tot negotiation, since the girl was really a young woman. She had Down syndrome. Moments later, as the carousel began, the mother wrapped her arms around her teen's waist, and she never let go. "You're doing a great job," she repeated several times.

I wondered whether I would behave differently when my own daughter became a teen. This was a good time to start.

After I lifted Talia onto a horse, I stepped down and stood outside the gate. Perched on her silver steed, she was all eyes and smiles as the carousel turned. You couldn't distinguish me from the other mothers who waved at their kids. In reality, I was vigilant—alert for any sign that Talia might get distracted and jump off the ride. Each time she circled by me, she waved with both her hands.

Later that day, we enjoyed a park picnic of pizza and chicken wings. Busy packing up, I failed to notice that Talia had left the picnic table. I turned and saw her perched in the branches of a nearby tree, 10 feet in the air.

"Mom, you have to get me down," she said. Grinning, feet swinging in the air, she was in no hurry to rejoin me.

"You can climb down all by yourself," I said. Swallowing another bite of pizza, I tried not to look.

She returned to our table smirking and pointing to a rip in her new shorts. But she was fine.

"Looks like the tree ate your shorts. You're a great climber," I said.

She giggled and looked straight into my eyes. In moments like these, the mischievous child who is Talia comes bursting out beyond the restraints of autism. She stands bearing the badges of an adventurer—ripped shorts, dirty hands, and grass-colored knees. She is strong, agile, and capable.

She scampered away again to climb trees and catch clouds. I let her go. I let her join the community of six-year-olds who leap and stretch without their mothers grabbing onto their waists—trying to bind them to the earth.

My daughter doesn't waste time turning to look for me. She knows that I'm nearby, enjoying my time in the sun.

The yellow slides in life are bumpy and unpredictable. But the ride is thrilling. And the burn mark on my daughter's wrist reminds me—sometimes I just have to let her go.

Amy Baskin

Snake Dreams

Parenting a child with autism is adventurous—tough, trying, and sometimes sad, but always an adventure. Perhaps one of the most challenging aspects for me has been learning how to handle fixations.

"Boy, he sure likes snakes," a voice says over my shoulder.

I turn to see a man I recognize, the father of Carolyn, a petite social butterfly in my son's first grade class. Her dad is a kind-looking man with a deep tan and long, sandy blonde hair tied in a ponytail at the back. He looks like a surfer and probably is.

"Oh," I say, looking over to my son, hard at work on a drawing of a large black snake. "You have no idea."

We are standing with the rest of the parents at the back of the room, waiting for class to end. Circle time is a nice way to wrap up the day, a chance for the kids to sit together and share, one on one, their favorite activity of the day. My son sits apart from the group, coloring quietly at his desk, doing his own thing.

Finally, the bell rings and chaos fills the room. Twenty squealing, giggling first-graders grab backpacks and greet parents and friends.

"Don't forget your homework folders. I'll see you all tomorrow!" the teacher yells above the din.

Within a few short minutes, the room is empty; it is so quiet, all I hear is the gentle squeak of the overhead ceiling fan. My son continues to work, unfazed by the change in the room.

"Wow! That's really terrific," I say, walking over to him.

He continues coloring, mind focused like a laser on the snake drawing in front of him.

"Is that a king cobra?" I ask, trying to catch his attention.

No answer. I sit down to wait, watching as he carefully selects a gold crayon from his color box to highlight the snake's flared hood.

My son is into snakes; I mean, totally hooked. Before snakes, it was Spider Man. And before that, it was Peter Pan. We had a long stretch of Peter Pan. But what passes as a normal interest for a typical child is much different than what my son experiences. He has Asperger's syndrome, and when he is hooked on something, he is totally fixated. My son's mind delves deep into subjects, perhaps to block out and escape the world and all its craziness—loud sounds, intense smells, or the crush of too many people. He dives deep, swallows details, and gulps down facts like comfort food.

So right now it's snakes. If I want to communicate with him and be in his world, this is what we talk about. I read books and tell bedtime stories in which the hero befriends a legless reptile or becomes one. I do this even though snakes freak me out. I do it all because I am his mother, and I love my son.

"Which snake is your favorite, Mommy? Today my favorite is the bushmaster. Tomorrow it might be the green tree python or maybe the Hawaiian blind snake. I can't decide yet. Mommy, what's your favorite today?"

The questions come at me with lighting speed. I can't get the answers out quickly enough for him, so he continues like a skip on a record player—"Mommy, what's your favorite snake today?"—again and again, until I finally manage to squeeze in an answer.

"I don't know, honey. I think I'm going with the rainbow boa." And I tell the truth. The rainbow boa is pretty, as snakes go. When light hits the outer scales of this colorful reptile, it splits like a prism, casting an iridescent sheen. Beautiful.

"Oh, that's a good one!" he says, nodding.

So it goes with my son and his snakes. Fixations can be difficult for a parent to handle. Years of experience have taught me to be more patient, but it wasn't always that way.

In the beginning, my husband and I tried to talk our son out of his obsessions, not understanding the strange pull certain items had on him. We encouraged him to play with other toys. We arranged play dates, hoping to interest him in playing with other children. We wanted desperately for him to fit in and to behave like normal kids do. We worried, *Is it healthy for him to obsess about things?* Our pediatrician, a sweet man with a snowy white beard, didn't think it was. Occupational therapists and school counselors were called in, but the efforts left everyone frustrated.

Today, we see that my son's fixations provide a place of calm for him—a mental hideaway where he can go when the world around becomes too much to handle. So I've made a type of mental truce with the fixations: We go with the flow, meet him where he is, and expect nothing less than for him to be the miracle child he is—snakes and all.

Just before bed, Snakeman went missing. The small green action figure with a snake's head is a favorite.

"Mommy, Snakeman is gone!"

"Did you look in the basket?" I ask. My hands are deep in a sink of soapy dishes.

"He's gone!" I see the look in his eyes and dry my hands. Dishes can wait. You see, my world stops when his does. It is the mother bear rising up in me, trying to make things right when I can. Right now, nothing is more important than to help my child.

We search high and low, but still no Snakeman. I feel desperation fill the room with unbearable intensity. He screams, eyes wild, frantic, unfocused.

"Honey?" I ask gently.

No answer. I am lost to him.

I put my hand on his shoulder. "Honey?"

Weeping now, his small face is twisted with anxiety. He lies on his bed, moaning. I hear pain, frustration, and a deep well of sorrow in his voice.

"We'll find him," I offer.

He runs from the room, whimpering and defeated, tears streaming down his face. I rip open the toy chest and search through drawers. Calling out with all my senses alive, "Snakeman, where are you?"

It is the mystery of autism—a lightning bolt of emotion and a desperate mother amid a room full of action figures . . . and still no Snakeman. Finally, I flip up the bed sheet and discover the missing hero at the bottom of the bed. I hold him up, like the Holy Grail.

"Here he is!" I yell, close to tears. "I have Snakeman!"

My son runs back into the room and wraps his arms around me. "Thank you, Mommy!"

He is elated; I am spent.

Later, after teeth are brushed and stories are read, I tuck my son and Snakeman safely into bed. I curl up with them and watch moonbeams play on the ceiling. Outside, the tropic wildlife welcomes the cool night air. Crickets chirp, and bullfrogs croak lullabies to the rustling palms. The trade winds are back. Somewhere in our yard, a Hawaiian blind snake makes his way along the grass, looking for a meal.

"Goodnight, honey," I say, kissing his sandy blond hair.

"Mommy?" His voice is a whisper. "I love you more than snakes."

Piper Selden

Moonlight

This is where we are now. It's an early September evening, and Will and I are sitting on a wooden bench beneath a crescent moon. The sky is black, the air is crisp and cool with the onset of autumn, and high up in the dark, the bright moon, hung at an angle, burns silver. We rest with our arms touching before a big fountain, the one that seemed such an unusual structure when it was first unveiled in the center of our upscale neighborhood shopping center a couple of years ago. It was designed to stand as an oasis amidst the buzzing palatial stores and quaint cafes that surround it. Now here it looms, a mini-Stonehenge with waterfalls, lit up like an attraction in the twilight. Will and I have learned to appreciate it, because the kids can actually play in it in summer, and on a night like tonight it soothes—it sings, as water spurts abundantly from the top of the big stones and splashes into the shining pool at their base.

The merchants are getting ready to lock their doors. We have already spent an hour or so inside the shops, not shopping, never shopping, but instead running all around as we always do. Mother chases boy, boy bumps into other boys who are picking out pencils in the school supplies section of the drug-store—boys who chatter away about which color notebook to buy, on this eve of the week before my boy's third grade life begins.

William simply cannot stand still in a school supplies aisle or in any other section of any place of business. He bounces off the walls, he "sharks," as his occupational therapist calls it—runs the inside perimeter of the building, moving round and round and round at rapid speed. There is too much stuff in a store, too much for his brain to handle. So the aisles are enough—the aisles and the doors and the exit signs are what he sees and knows—the things that guide him through the chaos. This racing through stores, which first began when Will was two (he is now nine), has become just a regular part of our lives, like a stroll in the park.

Our dip into the drugstore lasts a total of three or four minutes, and the same for all the other stores in the village of shops. Then, finally, here on the bench by the shimmering fountain, the chase is over, and the little shark relaxes. We are in the open air, in the calm night, and there is nothing to stimulate but cascading water and its burbling melody. We are alone in the moonlight.

The conversation, led by him, goes like this:

"Elementary school has fourth grade and fifth grade left to go." His green eyes stare up at Stonehenge, reflecting silver light, flashing with thoughts.

"Yes," I say.

"After that, we don't know what middle school I'm going to choose."

"Right."

He once drew a chart on his chalkboard of all the grades up through four years of college. Then he added: *Job—2 years.*

"It could be Hamilton or Eckstein." Will knows every last school building in the Seattle district. He's made his father and me drive past each one of them a hundred times. We've traipsed them on foot during off-hours, and we know every corner and cranny. It is the layout of each school campus that pulls him—the halls, the boys' and girls' bathrooms. Little variations on a design that is, when set apart from bustling hollering crowds of students, so beautifully predictable.

"Could be." I'm really listening now, after doing our store run on automatic pilot.

"Could be," Will echoes.

My heart is brought up short. If there happened to be anyone passing by, this little boy's manner of speaking would sound odd. It comes out in a funny singsong, so baby-like for a child his size. And the mother's voice in response might sound casual, like a normal mom talking to her kid. But, truthfully, the kid is at his shining, unprecedented best, and Mom is holding her breath. I am, as my soul starts to stir, trying to contain myself. This is a conversation. This is something that has been an incredible uphill battle for Will—something that we work hard every day to achieve. For years we've paid professionals to assist us with this. We've written stories about conversations to try to get one going. And now here it is, rolling along spectacularly, without struggle, the words sailing happily up into the luxuriant night air.

"After high school comes college."

This is a new one on me. "Yes, college," I say. "Maybe," I add quickly.

"I'll go to the University of Washington. I'll have my lunch in the Student Union building. I'll have a cookie, a muffin, or a scone."

Now I feel the need to interject and not for reasons of nutrition. "People have to pay a lot of money to go there, you know, Will. Lots of people are trying to get in. We'll see." Why can't I just let him dream on, a child's dream? It's because I know. He gets these things in his mind, and he is like no child or human I have ever seen. The thought forms in concrete and can't be moved. Once built, it stays and stays—until he graduates from high school and he's standing there confronting me as if no time had ever lapsed between this moment and the future. He'll be asking me then about the UW, I'm sure of it. But now the fall night crackles, and he goes on—disregarding my warning, and to my utter amazement.

"After that, I'll get a job. I'll live in an apartment down by the waterfront. I'll work at the Seattle Trade Center. I'll ride my bike."

Excellent! My concerns over how I'll create a private classroom at the UW vanish. I'm delighted with this design for a career track. I'm especially pleased that there is no car in it.

"I think there's a bike rack at the Trade Center," Yes, as a matter of fact, there probably is.

"I'll have an office . . . and a computer . . . and a view of the railroad tracks!" Certainly.

Now the scent of some faraway harvest-night bonfire rides past me on the breeze, and I am caught up. I snuggle into my sweater. This exchange is a miracle. I'm hearing about a dream—a dream!—from a boy whose way of thinking is so narrow and delayed it doesn't seem possible that a dream would be allowed in. And I'm imagining: The Trade Center. Can't one rent office space there? Couldn't I set something up?

"Maybe you'll even have an office door with your name on it!"

He scoots to the edge of the bench. "I'll have a sign that says, 'Will!'"

Everything in the shopping center is turned off, but the water in the fountain is still at play, tumbling and splashing in the spotlight, echoing Will's cry. So many nights I have lain awake as tears mixed with prayers dampened my pillow. I've put in a lot of time in the dark, feeling heavy and helpless and terrified for a future I can't predict. But suddenly, I've caught a glimpse of the future from the other side, and it's being held up before my eyes like an Olympic torch. Whatever has led us to this—years of speech therapy, hours upon hours of my own input based on instinct and a few educated guesses, his father's incredible talent for showing him a way to walk through this world—William can see his dream, and it looks good. In fact, it looks perfect. And he's telling me all about it.

Kelly Harland

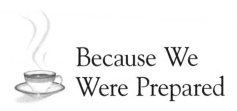

Because We Were Prepared

"Please, can I take the plunger in the stroller?" begged my four-year-old son, Jack. "Pretty please?"

Why would anyone want to take a toilet plunger for a walk?

My son's brain works in mysterious ways. The phrases "Asperger's" and "processing disorder" can't describe the inimitable and often beautiful way my son interprets the world around him. If it were up to me, I'd do away with the diagnosis of "processing disorder" and replace the term with "creative wiring." Jack's mind routes information through convoluted channels, with fascinating results. The same neural wiring that made it a trial for him to learn to speak, that led to a fifteen-minute crying jag when the rice cooker blew a fuse and had to be thrown away, that made him teary-eyed with sympathy at the struggles of Rowan Atkinson's "Mr. Bean," also gives him a unique perspective on problems that might seem insoluble to anyone else.

Most people, without realizing it, bow to social constraints in almost every decision they make. They allow emotion to cloud their judgment; they permit fear of falling behind the Jones's to guide their purchasing decisions; and they take peer pressure into account when they search for answers to their problems. My son, not having any concept of social mores or behaviors, is blissfully unfettered by them. His decisions are guided by logic and by solid problem-solving techniques, and nothing more.

So despite the bizarre nature of his request, I knew he must have a logical reason for wanting that plunger. Children with Asperger's, like my Jack, can be as logical as little Vulcans. The trick to understanding my son lies in learning to think in the same convoluted, yet logical, patterns. Some days I can do it, and some days I can't. This time, I was stumped.

I started to say no, but his pleading blue eyes and quivering lower lip did me in. It meant a lot to him. Who would it hurt? Did it really matter what the neighbors thought?

Last month, after learning that the oral sensitivity that made my son gag on certain foods might improve after a shaving-cream finger-painting session, we'd treated the neighbors to the sight of an adult woman and a little boy sitting in a driveway, foaming like rabid dogs. Then we'd added the sidewalk chalk to the mounds of shaving cream and scribbled until we discovered, to our horror, that the murals we were drawing had smeared like a bad watercolor. When we went inside, leaving behind the messy dregs of our efforts, we also left plenty of fodder for the neighborhood gossip mill.

And what about the morning my son woke up and announced that we had to build a submarine, and we'd spent the afternoon ankle-deep in the wading pool out front testing prototypes? And then there'd been the plastic grocery bag kite tied with yarn that worked surprisingly well until it tangled in the neighbor's lilac bush.

What about the day my son felt the need to put up "walk here" signs all along our sidewalk and "not here" signs on the grass? Our neighbors already had ample cause to believe insanity runs in our family. One plunger, more or less, wasn't going to make or break our reputation.

"All right," I told him, "You can bring the plunger, but we have to wash it first."

My son crowed with joy and ran to the bathroom closet.

At last the plunger was as clean as bleach could make it. Jack grabbed the wooden handle, wielding the object of his desire like a broadsword, and climbed into his stroller. "Hurry, Mommy!" he said, "Find a hill! Quick!"

Completely baffled, I tucked his blanket around him, and we set off, keeping our eyes peeled for the first steep rise on our route.

Taking a plunger for a walk is a great way to scatter sunshine. The grumpy old man on the corner broke into an unprecedented smile. A man on a bicycle waved and laughed out loud, craning his neck after he'd passed. A woman walking her dog was so amused that she didn't notice she'd wandered off the sidewalk and into someone else's flower garden. And my son, for once not upset about the inconsistent route, the changing weather, or the unreliable blue of the sky, beamed the brightest.

When we reached the first hill, my son began bouncing up and down in his seat. "Go there, Mommy!" he shouted, pointing to the curb.

When we reached the sidewalk's edge, the stroller wheels rolling along in the gutter, Jack leapt into action. Slamming the rubber "business end" of the plunger onto the sidewalk ahead of us, he strained until the muscles in his skinny arms stood out, trying to get a good seal on the concrete. When the plunger's rubber bowl didn't cling to the concrete the way he expected it to, he lifted his plunger, brushed off the dust around the rim, and tried again, undaunted.

At last the pieces of the puzzle came together in my mind, and I understood why he was so deter-mined to bring the plumber's helper in his stroller that morning. My son had watched his mother huff and puff on the hills for weeks. He felt sorry for me. He'd consulted that creative brain of his and decided the toilet plunger was the answer to my problem. The plunger propulsion method worked for Wile E. Coyote when he wanted to climb up the cliff face, right? Why shouldn't it work for us? Simple logic.

Up the hill we went—my son pleased and proud, plunging away, doing his best to lever us up the sidewalk, and I laughing so hard I had to lean on the stroller's handlebar to stay upright. The morning commuters waved, honked, and laughed along with me.

At last we reached the top of the hill, where I thanked my gallant young son for his kindness and perception. Then I took a route home that had a few more hills. Because we were prepared.

Heather Jensen

Between the Lines

A horrible commotion was taking place on stage. The pantomime had come to a halt; the producer was wringing her hands; and everyone in the audience was on their feet. The performance of "Jack and the Beanstalk" was being completely disrupted by the twelve-year-old boy playing Jack . . . and I couldn't have been more pleased or proud.

It was my son up there in the spotlight, in front of all these people, in the lead role of Jack. And I knew I would never, ever forget this moment.

Exactly a dozen years to the day before his stage debut, Tim made his dramatic entrance into the world. It had been a normal pregnancy that ended with an emergency cesarean section. Having lost a serious amount of blood during the delivery of my second child, and only son, I had spent some time in intensive care afterward.

Tim had been worth it all. He was a cherubic, blond-haired, blue-eyed baby boy, with the longest dark eyelashes we'd ever seen. When we brought our beautiful baby boy home, where his two-year-old sister, Natalie, had been eagerly awaiting his arrival, our family was complete.

He met all his major milestones early. He walked at nine months, and by his first birthday, he had discernible names for each of his parents and sister and several words for our cat ("Lady," her name, "cat," and "meow"). We were proud and grateful parents of two wonderful children and probably did more than our fair share of boasting.

I cannot now pinpoint when I first realized he was losing his language. All I know is that I took him to the doctor when he was eighteen months old to ask for a hearing test, because I feared he was deaf. We could shout his name, and he just didn't respond. It turned out his hearing was fine; it was autism that had pulled our son into his own world.

I knew nothing about autism then, so it took a while before we realized the implications of what was happening. At three years old, he was given a diagnosis of pervasive developmental delay (PDD), and we were told that, though Tim might never learn to speak again, he might possibly learn to read. I was so thrilled by this, the first positive news we'd been given, that I burst into tears of sheer joy right there in the doctor's office.

Over the years, he has had sixteen additional diagnoses, but autism remains his greatest challenge.

Regardless of the prognosis and dire predictions we were given, I never gave up on Tim. I spoke to him all the time. I sang him nursery rhymes that I adapted to use his name and the names of his family, his home, and his town. I pointed out and named things to him on every journey we made; never minding that he always sat silently behind me, oblivious to his surroundings. Once on a visit to the dentist, I spent the entire car trip enthusing about passing buses, a fire truck, and a field of cows; only when I arrived at my destination and turned to unstrap my son from his car seat did I remember he was at home with a sitter.

My husband's work kept him away from home for long hours and sometimes took him out of town for days at a time. Tending to both children fell almost entirely to me, severely testing my energy and inner resources. Natalie was a very bright and gregarious child. By age two, she had memorized the alphabet and all her storybooks, word for word. It was impossible to skip even one word of a bedtime story. She never slept more than four hours in any twenty-four. Tim didn't sleep even that much and certainly never at the same time as Natalie. Sleep-deprived, stressed, and stretched to my limits trying to keep up with Natalie and to pacify Tim, I was an utter wreck.

I was only forty-two the first time a hairdresser asked if I'd come in for their "senior special" rates. I was so groggy from lack of sleep that I didn't even think to take the offered discount and instead indignantly insisted on paying the full price.

By the time Tim was four, he was a very angry and volatile child, and much of his angst and outbursts stemmed from his inability to communicate. I was certain that, in his head, he knew exactly what he wanted to say. But he had verbal dyspraxia and was almost unintelligible. Every word he spoke began with either d or n, since he was unable to enunciate any other consonant. No wonder he was enraged! Even I, his mother, couldn't understand more than a dozen of his words. And no wonder he took it out on his sister—by biting her so hard he drew blood—and by kicking my shins (the scars are still so bad that I don't ever wear short skirts, even in the hottest summers). He used to arch his back and throw himself backward in a tantrum, smashing his skull against the floor, paying no attention whether the surface was carpeted or tiled.

Our first breakthrough came when I took him to a cranial osteopath. For once, someone outside the family was comfortable being near him. If he crawled under her desk or treatment couch, she followed him. At first, he wouldn't let her touch his head, so she worked on his spine instead.

One day she announced that it had been a particularly good session. Within three days, he was counting up to ten. The words were still garbled—the verbal dyspraxia was overpowering. But for the first time, I had proof he'd understood our words all the while and was able to communicate—there was an active brain inside his always active body.

Together we counted, over and over again: "Du, doo, dee, dor, dy, di, de-de, day, ni, de." We lined up his metal trains, and we counted them. We lined up his cars and counted those, too.

Then, just two days later we were driving to the grocery story when he pointed for the first time and said, "De da."

"Tractor?" I asked, while scanning the parking lot and the road nearby for the vehicle he loved. It took a while, and it almost involved another tantrum as he repeated "de da" over and over to his uncomprehending mother. Finally I realized what he was pointing at—and that he had put together two words for the first time: red car.

We went round the entire parking lot, with him calling out "de da" or "dee da," naming all the different colored cars. And I wept with sheer happiness. We never did get around to doing the shopping that day, but we did create another memorable moment that will last a lifetime.

Tim's was a very literal world. I once gave him paints, brushes, and paper, and then showed him a die-cast model train and instructed him to paint the train, hoping to keep him amused while I concentrated (for once) on his sister. I still have the photo of the train he showed me a few minutes later—the metal model, dripping with many different paints—as he beamed a proud smile.

Another time I shouted at Tim to "Come down here now!"—without first checking to see exactly where he was. Turned out he was perched in a cardboard box at the top of the staircase. Faithful to my instructions, he launched himself and the box down the stairs, screaming as he hit every stair along the way. The cardboard box was a write-off, but by some miracle, Tim had only minor bruises.

When he was younger, Tim couldn't understand the concept of belongings. If he saw something he wanted, he just took it. When we'd tell him that was wrong, he just didn't get it. "Tim's now," he'd tell us, clutching the purloined object.

When the time came, Tim entered a mainstream school. He started off in their special needs unit, but soon he was integrating so well that at age seven he was asked to leave so that another child might have his place. For the first time ever, he was holding his own with "normal" children, albeit with a support worker.

Over the years, his confidence blossomed, and his intelligence began to shine through. He was placed in the top groups for science and math, and then, to our surprise, in English.

And so we approached his twelfth birthday.

Tim is now a member of a youth club called PHAB (PHysically-challenged and Able-Bodied children), which meets weekly. Recently PHAB auditioned actors for a pantomime. Tim insisted on auditioning and gave such a stunning performance (falling to his knees to plead, "Oh, mother, don't make me take the cow to market!") that he won the part of Jack.

Painstakingly, we went over his lines until he knew every one, and he seemed to have more lines than all the other cast members put together. We went over the need to project his voice and to turn to the audience as he spoke. We rehearsed his solo song. We explained that his costume in act one had to be ragged and patched; after all, Jack being disadvantaged was the point of the play. Since the play was to be held on his birthday, we offered to have his party the day afterward, something he seemed to understand and accept. I thought I had covered everything.

Then came the day of the performance—in front of a host of paying customers in our local theater. The first acts went well. Tim remembered all his lines, looked out at the audience, and spoke up, giving a dramatic performance, just as he had rehearsed.

The final act began well, too. But then—oh, no!—as the pantomime neared its climax, our boy "Jack" brought the entire performance to a halt. He stood there and calmly and loudly told the producer (as she stood anxiously in the wings) that he simply could not do what he was meant to do. Chaos ensued. While the cast of almost fifty children fretted back-stage, the producer came out onto the stage to urge Tim to continue. To no avail. The audience muttered their disapproval. The producer pleaded again. And still he refused. He stood there, holding his ground, with his arms crossed.

"I cannot do it," he told us all. "I will not take the harp from the giant!"

My heart was pounding. What would happen? I knew Tim was not a child who could be won over easily. Once he made up his mind, it stayed made up.

"I will not take it," he told us, "because it is wrong to steal."

There was total silence.

Then, from the back, came the sound of one person applauding. Another joined in, and another, and then the whole audience was on its feet, clapping and cheering. Pandemonium!

I was laughing and crying at the same time, and I wasn't alone. My autistic child had understood our world and shown us all a truth. It is a moment that I will never, ever forget.

Caroline M. Praed

Dancing with Puddles

"Want to go for lunch, Anthony?" I asked. He headed for the door. "You have to put your socks and shoes and a rain jacket on first. And you have to wait for Mommy."

After four days of endless rain, the walls of the hotel room felt like they were closing in. The girls had gone off to window shop, looking for cool guys and the forbidden, but trendy, nose rings. My fiancé, David, and I had taken Anthony to many local attractions, but the beach we knew he'd love was too cold in this weather. Anthony was getting bored. His frequent and persistent autistic noises—somewhere between a calf's bellow and an elephant's roar—were getting on David's nerves. A part of our lives for only two years, David was still getting used to parenting a child with autism. He was starting to feel overwhelmed. It was time to give him a break.

I got ready in a flash. I had to. Once Anthony's shoes and jacket were on, he'd be gone. I couldn't take the chance he might sprint down the hallway and onto the elevator. Who knew how long it would take to find him if he slipped out on another floor, or worse, into the lobby, then onto the street? My child loose on the street in a strange city, with no traffic smarts and no verbal skills, was a terrifying possibility. A dash of lipstick and a hastily donned rain jacket later, I managed to catch Anthony just before the elevator, and we headed down to the wet street.

The rain was pelting down, but Anthony was in his glory. He moved up the busy downtown street puddle by puddle. Puddles on the sidewalk, puddles on the street, puddles in the alleyways and in the entries to stores, drips from the awnings overhead—it didn't matter to Anthony. He simply followed their course, making his very excited noise as he went.

I was not as carefree. I wanted to be having fun with Anthony and to give him the space even an eleven-year-old with autism needs. But every time he stepped off the curb into a puddle, I'd end up barking, "Get off the street, Anthony," and guiding him back onto the sidewalk. Or I'd tell him, "That's enough time with this puddle. People need to get by." Or "The drips from the awning are really neat, aren't they? They make lots of circles in the puddles, but we have to move out of the way. These people need to get into the store."

In his characteristic way, Anthony would cross his index fingers, press them against his left nostril, gnaw on his right knuckle, and make his grating noise. I'd explain the situation to him again, trying to be respectful of the processing time he needed, painfully aware that the waiting pedestrians weren't likely to be that patient.

Relax, Deb, I told myself. *Anthony needs to have fun. Give him some space.* I'd try to slow myself to Anthony's pace, allowing him time to enjoy this puddle and then dart to the next one.

"Anthony! Move!" I shouted. "The car in that alley needs to get on the street." Anthony was oblivious to the vehicle he was blocking as he focused on the "brown clouds" in the puddles.

"Anthony, move over!" Pedestrians couldn't possibly know the child racing straight for them would veer out of their way only at the last possible second. I'd catch up and physically redirect him, wondering what the people must be thinking. Despite my attempts to let Anthony have fun, I was feeling more like a drill sergeant than a caring mom and, worse, a target for the judgment of others.

Up the street, I noticed a woman—another pedestrian—older and respectably dressed. We'd passed her by in our quest for puddles. Then she had passed us as Anthony stopped to splash. She'd been eyeing us, and I wondered what she was thinking.

Now we were all at a street corner, where I tried to keep Anthony on the curb until it was safe to cross. I felt defensive. Was she judging Anthony? Was she judging me?

Just at that moment, the woman looked toward us and caught my eye. "You are blessed," she said to me. Nothing more, just, "You are blessed." The light changed, and she continued on her way, leaving me dumbfounded as Anthony and I continued our slow dance with puddles.

"You are blessed." The words rang in my ears. Never before had a stranger (other than the Hare Krishna street-corner types of my teen years) stopped me on a street corner to tell me I was blessed. Never before had someone who had clearly observed the interaction between Anthony and me felt compelled to say such a thing.

"You are blessed." I rolled the words around in my mouth, tasting them, feeling the way they settled my body. Me? Blessed? I pondered this as Anthony and I ate lunch in a warm little bistro, and something opened inside me that seemed to transcend the worry, the hyper-vigilance, and the self-condemnation.

Sometimes, I think that holiday and those puddles are metaphors for life with Anthony. We had expected a sun-filled week at the beach. Instead, it rained steadily. I had expected a healthy child. Instead, my son developed autism. Anthony and his autism have taken me on a path I wouldn't have chosen, a path that's put me in many situations I couldn't anticipate. But just like our journey up that puddle-filled street, there have been unexpected blessings.

The blessings are seldom in the still waters or down the easy paths. They are in the challenges that arise and get resolved. They are in learning how to respond to problems and how to find inner strength, endurance, courage, new skills and talents, and new, often unforeseen, relationships that help us respond creatively to the challenges Anthony's autism brings. Puddles get stirred up, but they settle back down. Rainy days—even rainy weeks—ultimately give way to sunshine.

My puddle-jumping boy is now a handsome young man of seventeen who shaves, goes to high school, and has crushes on girls. He still presses his crossed index fingers to his left nostril and makes his noise—less frequently, thankfully, but somewhat louder now that his voice has deepened. His verbal skills have grown enough that he can let us know some basic needs and wants—something I was afraid might never happen.

The inner conflict I'd endured when encouraging Anthony to have fun while respecting others' needs has paid off. Anthony now participates in many community activities—grocery shopping, work experience, movies, even dining in fine restaurants—with minimal disruption. He's even had a date! He has maintained his gentle disposition, and, in the past two years, has taken to giving me kisses several times a day. There has been struggle, and there has been joy. I suspect there will be more of both when Anthony turns eighteen and legally becomes an adult this spring.

Over the years I've come to terms with Anthony's autism. It no longer seems to matter. It takes only a glimpse of his face in repose to see his sweet soul shining through, and I realize again what that woman on the puddled street saw in an instant—I am truly blessed.

Deborah Barrett-Jardine

Lunar Eclipse

"Tell me when it's the bottom of the ninth," I shout from my desk in the breakfast nook.

"You just want to see the part where the guys jump on each other, all happy and excited." My younger son, Thomas, shouts from upstairs, where he's cheering the Red Sox on television.

His brother is watching the same game, but rooting for the Cardinals, in the living room. At nine and eleven, Thomas and Ben can't sit on the couch together without bickering and poking each other—even when it's not baseball season.

Thomas is right. I am drawn to the end of competitions, when players finally unmask and release pent-up emotions, when they let us see joy, a mass ecstasy, so intense it's almost frightening. I love it when they grab each other in wild embraces and hop in circles, or fall to their knees and sob. And when some of them point to the sky and mouth the words "Thank you," even though I'm not religious, I'm moved.

When Ben calls me to watch the last few minutes of the World Series, I join him on the couch in the living room, shifting sideways to stretch my legs. One of my feet grazes his ankle, and he winces.

"Owie. Hurtie," he says in the middle school baby talk he and several of his friends use. It fits them perfectly. Inside those pubescent bodies, they are still toddlers.

Because he can't tolerate even a light touch, he tries to push my feet away. But because I sometimes wonder if he needs to toughen up, I leave them where they are.

"No, no. No touchy. Better if no touchy."

I dangle my legs over the side of the couch. "Why can't I just stretch out for a minute? Put my feet in your lap?"

Just when I think things are going well, just when I think we may have this madness beat, that we're on the cusp of outwitting the sensory integration disorder and the Asperger's, just when I convince myself that he will outgrow it or we're past the worst, we are humbled again. Its pull on us—like that of the moon—is too strong.

The Red Sox make the third out, and Thomas chants from upstairs. "Oh yeah, Bosox are the champs."

Ben and I watch a few minutes of the post-game interviews, but players are only shouting into microphones, and no one's crying, so I turn it off.

"Time to brush teeth, sweet boy." I wonder if this will be a battle tonight; he's tired and getting over a cold, both precursors to a meltdown. "Let's check the eclipse again, and then you need to get to bed."

The last tantrum, six months ago, ended in his smashing a framed print in the dining room. It began with the word no. That day, with Thomas off at a soccer game, Ben wanted to play computer games before taking out the trash. I said no. He argued. I said no. He fell apart. "I want to play the computer now! Are you deaf?" He waved his hand in front of my face as if I were temporarily blind rather than deaf.

"Go to your room now. You have a ten-minute time-out."

"Why?"

"We can talk about it after your time-out." I kept my voice low—my hypnotic voice, I call it—praying I could somehow circumvent the blow-up. But I knew it was probably too late; we were too far into the meltdown.

"You always say that, and you never do."

"Go," I said, pointing toward his room.

"Why? W-h-y? Do you understand English?"

He stomped his foot, his face deep claret. This was the pattern, the loop he got trapped in. He was crying, tears spilling onto his shirt. The volume still surprised me.

"You're stuck, Ben," I said. "Go to your room now to calm down, or you'll be grounded tomorrow."

If I can get him to his room, it means we're in the final stage of the meltdown. He'll pound on his floor and sob into his pillows. Then he'll cry softly, moaning about how unfair and mean I am. Then it will be over. My sweet boy will be back.

"Why? Can't you just answer that question, or are you too stupid?"

"You're grounded tomorrow." I shouted to be heard over his ranting, his chanting. I should have stayed calm, concealed my anger, but I didn't like being called stupid. Sometimes the most inane words get to me. They push past my calm exterior, ignite something inside me.

"Why am I grounded tomorrow?" he shouted.

I headed to the kitchen, thinking maybe he'd stop sooner without an audience. But instead of giving up, his shouting became louder; he followed me, screaming, stomping his feet, still demanding. "I want computer time now. Can't you hear me? Or are you an idiot?"

Needing something to do, I filled a glass of water from the tap. I had to get away from the irritation, the noise, his noise, which was buzzing around in my head, my own sensory overload eclipsing the equilibrium I'd been feeling lately. He hadn't had a tantrum in weeks.

Before I could take a sip of the water though, I turned and found him right behind me, his body too close, his voice bouncing off the linoleum floor and pine cabinets, his tone threatening to flay me. Taking a step forward, I tossed the water from the glass at him. I wanted to shock him, wake him from the trance, make him stop the noise and shake his head like a dog after a bath. I wanted him to realize his mistake, apologize, and retreat to his room. Give us both a rest. Like in the movies, I wanted the water in the face to be a wake-up call, a shocking but harmless way to halt the scene. Just make it stop.

But the water didn't reach his face; I was too far away and didn't use enough force to jettison the half-cup of liquid that high. I could see its path during the seconds it was airborne, like a freeze frame, before it left its trajectory, broke apart, and landed on his shirt. At the same time I tossed the water I thought, *What the hell am I doing? This was not a drunk who had insulted me at a party, this was my eleven-year-old son who did not deserve this, did not deserve a mother who came unraveled and turned into a terrifying witch when she could no longer cope.*

Ben stalked to the refrigerator, where he grabbed what I thought was a plastic bottle of water to pour on the floor to match my gesture. But it was a jug of apple juice, and before I could reach him, he unscrewed the lid and shook the jug, spraying apple juice all over the linoleum, the stove, and the cabinets.

"Stop it," I screamed. "Stop it, stop it, stop it!"

He dropped the jug, stomped to his room, and slammed his fist into the wall, smashing the framed print in the dining room when he passed it.

I tossed rags from under the sink on the puddle of apple juice and stepped out of the kitchen. He could clean it up later. At least it was over. I would call the family therapist in the morning.

Hands still trembling, I began tidying the dining room, removing papers from the table, straightening the clutter on the sideboard. Trying to put things back in order.

On the couch now, six months later, the baseball game is over, and it's time for bed. Ben clambers like a Godzilla-sized spider to my end of the couch. I brace for his favorite trick—pretending he's about to fall on me but catching himself at the last minute. I hate this trick, because I'm afraid he'll slip, and I'll end up with an elbow in my eye. But instead, he lies on his side, squeezing next to me on the narrow couch, resting his head in the cradle between my shoulder and neck. Ben is large for his age, long and burly. His body, only inches shorter than mine, presses into my side with startling abandon, and his solid torso warms me. His bare feet, which had recoiled at my touch moments before, are now entwined with mine. His scalp is so near my lips I have only to lean an inch to reach him. His hair, the texture of straw from swimming, needs to be washed, but I kiss his head three times in the same spot, above his temple.

Maybe the dark phase is finally over. Maybe we've left the worst times behind. Maybe his teen years will be fun. I want to believe this so badly, but I know it's lunacy. When are the teen years ever fun for parents? At least now we recognize pretantrum behavior, can sometimes thwart meltdowns.

"Poor thing," I say. "Are you sad because your team didn't win?" I'm joking, but he doesn't respond.

He was the only one in the family rooting for the Cardinals, the whole series is over now, and it's time for bed.

"No. The Giants are my team," he says, smiling.

I kiss his head over and over, until I remember this will likely drive him away. Then I lie absolutely still, eager to prolong this moment, with my son's entire body clamped to mine, becalmed.

"I remember when you were a little baby, and I was lying right here on this couch, and I laid you on my chest and—

"—The As are my second team," he says. "And then the—"

"Come on," I say, "Let me reminisce for a minute. You were only this big." I hold one hand at my waist and the other at my neck. "Not this huge ol' long kid you are now."

"Oh, Mommy." He gives me only a moment to hold onto the memory. And I do remember binding him snuggly in a receiving blanket, the baby burrito I called him, how he sucked my pinkie until it puckered up like a topographical map. "I wanted the Cardinals to win because the Red Sox made it instead of the Giants, and the Cardinals haven't won—"

"You always root for the underdog, don't you?"

I'm grasping his back with firm pressure in two spots, one hand cupping a shoulder blade, the other holding his lower back like a dance partner, bearing down as if he'll float away. Unlike his brother, a sensory sponge, I am allowed to touch my eldest only rarely, and I fear each time will be the last. I'm careful not to breathe on him; I want this to last forever.

He rises to one elbow, and for a second I think he's simply readjusting his position, getting more comfortable, but in the next moment he has hopped off the couch and bounced away. "I have to check the eclipse," he says, grabbing his clipboard from the coffee table. Then he leaves through the front door to draw this stage of the total lunar eclipse, before it begins to wane.

Anne Clark

How the Goose
Saved Christmas

"That's it," I declared, facing down my husband. "We're getting a dog."

It had been an on-again, off-again discussion for months. The entire time, our three kids had all been fervently pro, my husband had been soundly con, and I had wavered like a bowl of Jell-O.

I was aware of the difficulties involved, of course, but frankly, I was not willing to confront another flock of geese. My mind was made up: We were definitely getting a dog.

My daughters hadn't always liked dogs. In fact, both of them started out life terrified of them. But as time went on, the furry guys had clearly grown on them. They were willing to take the plunge.

Andrew, our autistic son, however, has always loved dogs. Since he was an infant, his cherubic, Down syndrome face has lit up at the sight of any canine in the vicinity. Once when he was five, he ran a full block in order to get to a dog. It was a new dog, one we'd never seen before, but the owner graciously allowed Andrew to pet (read: lie across with full body) her little terrier. Then, alas! As the woman led away her pup, we caught sight of Spike the golden retriever just leaving with his owner on the opposite side of the park. Desperate to get to Spike, Andrew booked it across the park in record time in order to greet his beloved and profusely shedding friend.

Mind you, Andrew was not known to have extraordinary endurance at the time. In fact, only a few weeks later, his school team made running fifty feet one of his IEP (Independent Education Program) goals.

"He can do that already, you know," I pointed out. The entire team—teacher, special education teacher, physical therapist, occupational therapist, speech therapist, and gym teacher—looked askance at me. "Surely not," their unified expressions read.

"Put a dog at the end of that fifty feet, and I assure you, he will run it every time," I insisted.

Comprehension dawned. What I was saying clicked. The woman has something there, they recognized.

Andrew's delight in—and some might say, obsession with—dogs was as well known as his fascination with elephants. Not too many elephants frequented the local parks, though, so Andrew's enthusiasm had always been directed to the dog population . . . until the day he found the geese.

Our neighborhood was graced with a number of well-equipped parks, and we liked to visit them each in turn. One park had a playground right next to the street, but the grounds included a long vacant field and a lake. Following the unspoken but never-broken rule of swings first, I'd struck up a conversation with another mom as I pushed Andrew and Lauren, my youngest, on the swings. After a while, the park routine exhausted (swings, monkey bars, slide, swings again), Andrew contented himself for a while exploring the no-mans-land of the grassy field, while Lauren rediscovered sand. All seemed quiet on the western front, so I returned to my conversation with the other mother, always grateful, as I was in those days, for a chance at adult conversation.

I kept my eyes on Andrew as the other mom and I chatted. He seemed to be intrigued with something, but I couldn't tell what. I watched as he wandered around in the grass, and since he wasn't dangerously close to the water, I let him.

Suddenly, the object of Andrew's interest became clear. A loud honk filled the air just as Andrew broke into that beautiful run that he'd demonstrated a few weeks earlier at the other park. Mid-sentence, I'm sure, I took off at a dead run to intercept Andrew's clear intention of petting (again, read: lie down upon) a goose.

I had always assumed that in a life-threatening situation I would discover that some kind of amazing super-human ability would set in. Like if, say, a bus fell over on top of one of my babies, Popeye-like brawn would pop out in places I didn't know I had. I would somehow manage—straining, no doubt, but still manage—to lift the bus and save my child. Alas, I must confess that this illusion held no water, at least not in this case. The last one picked for every kickball game at Cooper Elementary, I have been notoriously slow all my life. Goose emergencies, sadly, were apparently no exception. In a dream-like fog, I ran toward my son, who was running toward a goose, who was running toward him. I was, undoubtedly, the slowest one of the bunch (flock?).

"Andrew, no!" I screamed. But Andrew was too excited about his new friend to hear what I was yelling. Bear in mind that Andrew rarely turned to his own name in those days, anyway, and if the word "no" got any response at all, it always seemed like a particularly funny joke to the boy. I would either have to pick up the pace or somehow communicate to the goose to buzz off. I didn't see a whole lot of hope for either of those possibilities, so I just kept running.

I quickly realized why the goose was so hostile, apart from just being a goose. It was standing in front of a bunch of smaller gooses—goslings, if you will–and was protecting his family, of course. Stretching out his considerable wings, the gander opened its beak (bill?) wide, and, correct me if I'm wrong, but I could have sworn it hissed at my son. Had it been possible, I think the creature would have donned black leather and pulled a switchblade. I mean, this goose looked mean.

I reached Andrew with about 6 feet separating him from the goose. The goose had stopped running by then and was frozen in a protective stance with his head lowered and continuing to hiss. I grabbed Andrew's hand and started pulling him away. Andrew, who had still been hoping to get better acquainted with the geese, was not keen to run the opposite direction. After only a few feet, he managed to trip over his dragging feet, and he fell.

The goose, seeing that our exit had stalled, felt he'd better clarify his position. With a renewed hiss and a winged charge, he did just that. I believe I said something like, "Aaaaaaargh!" Andrew laughed.

With somewhat less gentleness than I might normally display, I jerked Andrew to his feet and beat it out of Goosetown. I'm not sure how much Andrew was cooperating at that point, but I knew one thing was for sure: I was not going to stick around to see what comes after a hiss and a charge. We were out of there—and we were definitely getting a dog.

In retrospect, I'm glad we ran into the geese (or nearly) It's Christmas Eve, and it's been a hard night for Andrew. We never go to church at night, but tonight we did. We never light candles in the dark sanctuary, but tonight we did. We never come home and open presents, but tonight we did.

Most kids love Christmas. For Andrew, Christmas is one colossal break in the routine of life. It comes with just too many unknowns, too much pressure. I know what he means. I love the baby Jesus, but I don't really like all the hullabaloo of Christmas.

It's bedtime, and Andrew is worn out. As I offer him a selection of bedtime stories, he pushes the familiar tales aside. Clapping his hands, he calls Barney, his big oaf of a yellow lab up on the bed.

Barney is a key part of Andrew's life now. My son is responsible for his dog, and he feeds, walks, and brushes him regularly. In a way, Barney redefines Andrew; in this one area, it is Andrew who is the caregiver. No longer is he always the one cared for. Like Andrew, Barney communicates best visually, and for once Andrew's lack of verbalizations don't hinder his ability to communicate. Barney, a young and vibrant lab, isn't easy to ignore. We've noticed that since Barney's joined our family, Andrew is more likely to make eye contact and turn to his name. Barney is far more than a pet. He is a therapy dog.

I am so grateful for Barney on days like these. With muffled Christmas carols still playing in the other room, Andrew lays his head on Barney's side, eyes hollow and exhausted by the day, and wraps an arm around his dog's face. Barney proceeds to lick Andrew's hand and to calm the seven-year-old boy. His big warm body offers the sensory input my son craves—no, needs. And gently, Barney soaks up all of the holiday tension and allows Andrew to finally rest.

Thank God for the grumpy goose.

Dena Fox Luchsinger

The Pray Grounds

oth arms rock back and forth several times—slowly, deliberately. My left hand settles into the glove, lightly gripping the baseball. I step back with my right foot, turn my left, kick the right, and then thrust all my weight forward, left knee bent, my body's entire weight folding behind my left arm as the ball is released toward home plate.

I am seven years old. I'm good. Small for my age (third in line up of my second grade class), I don't have much of an arm from the outfield, but I've got a good glove, a good stick, decent range.

But most of all, I have experience. My father started me early. From the time I was four, we went to the parade grounds every Sunday morning, weather permitting, or the "pray" grounds, as I thought them to be called.

These memories come flooding back now as I cross the outfield grass, toward diamond two. I'm in sunny Los Angeles, the Westside, no less—manicured grass, smooth brown infield dirt, baselines. I'm not in Brooklyn anymore.

My wife signed up our son for Little League. How could she know? She hadn't played ball. She couldn't know its potential for being brutal, mean, unforgiving. Kids get quick, devastating messages on Little League fields. A single snide comment, a chuckle, or a laugh at your expense can permanently scare you off the hard-fought streets, away from the schoolyards, from stickball, Chinese handball, paddle ball, relegating you to a life of riding your bicycle from a distance and joining the school orchestra.

This is not a place for a kid whose body betrays him, for a kid who, at seven, can't tie his shoes yet, who looks awkward and gangly in his clean, white uniform. This is not a place for fragile kids with sensitive souls.

I see my wife. She smiles at me gratefully for leaving work early, for being there. She's worried. She whispers that she spoke earlier in the day to our son's physical therapist, who thought this was a bad idea, that our son would never be able to judge the flight of a ball through air. The knot in my stomach grows tighter. I smile at her, reassuringly.

"It'll be fine," I say. I'm terrified.

Looking out at the diamond, I return to the world of childhood sports, of dashed hopes and dreams, of moments of greatness, battles won and lost, and I realize how loaded all this is for me. I watch with envy the kids already out on the field, joyfully flinging the ball around like it was what they were born to do—what my kid should look like out there.

My son stands on the field, looking around vaguely, out of position, in some Neverland between short and third, only occasionally looking toward home plate as the kids take batting practice. I yell out desperate directives to him, as quietly and inconspicuously as possible: "Look at the batter." "Bend your knees." "Put your glove back on." "Stand up."

A ground ball comes right toward him. My heart pounds. I put my hand down, hoping desperately that he will put his glove down too. The ball goes right through his legs. A kid next to him runs back and picks up the ball; throws it back into the infield.

The next thing that happens is my son begins to cry. I watch him, momentarily unable to move, as time slows down, like when you're in a car accident. I'd like to say this is a little sniffle. But what we have is a full-on episode of gasping-for-air, snot-producing weeping.

I literally carry him off the field. There is nothing vaguely athletic about any of this. I sit, holding my son in his baseball uniform on my lap as he weeps snotty tears into my shirt. We are in the dugout. The dugout. A holy ground reserved for spitting, strategizing, cussing, and manly fits of rage. There doesn't seem to be any sign of this ending. I wonder what people are thinking. The parents, the other kids. The coach. I imagine them all dreading that they got stuck with this kid on their team.

Here are things I don't say to my son: "Buck up." "Baseball players don't cry." "Stop acting like a baby."

Our family has had too much therapeutic pre-school for that. When he is finally able to speak, he explains to me that he wasn't upset because he missed the ball but because the other boy ran and took it from him. I explain to him that's what happens in baseball. You back up the other players. He was helping you. He was being a teammate.

My son wants to leave. I remind him that Mommy signed him up. "Unsign me up," he demands.

Admittedly, this idea sounds alluring. We could do it, couldn't we? Walk away. Go home. Never put on a baseball uniform again. I enjoy a brief, delicious moment of self pity. Why couldn't I have a normal kid? A kid I could bestow my endless baseball wisdom onto. A kid I could take out to a field and hit ground-balls to? How can I be denied carrying on this gentle, profound, poetic legacy?

When the weeping is over, I remind my son that he seemed to be having some fun out there and that if we walk away he might miss out. I tell him that I played baseball as a kid and had a lot of fun. I put the decision in his hands, knowing the odds are incredibly high that we will soon be walking away, just as we have walked away from so many things over the course of his young life. He routinely walks away from anything that has a large group of people, anything that requires waiting, and until recently, any place where there was a candle or any kind of fire. Zoos, fairs, museums, parades. The list goes on.

Then it happens. To this day, I don't know why. He gets off my lap and marches back out onto the field. He stays for the whole practice.

Days later, I come home from work, and he is watching a baseball game on television. He seems involved. At dinner, he starts asking me questions. "What's a run?" "What's a curve ball?" "How do you win?" I answer the questions with a tone of nonchalance, fearing that if he detects an ounce of enthusiasm, all interest will immediately fizzle.

A couple of days later, I suggest we go out and play catch. My wife and I make many suggestions. Let's play catch; let's walk to town; let's see a movie. Our suggestions are often not met with a great deal of enthusiasm. It's as though my wife and I are teenage boys desperately trying to woo a girl who has absolutely no interest. He's not a big fan of the unfamiliar. He likes what he likes.

For some unknown reason, he agrees. We go to the backyard. He throws the ball to me. I give him a few simple directives. Put your right hand near your ear; bend your elbow; step in with your left foot; throw right into my glove. He wings the ball under-hand, with a spastic, uncoordinated motion. It lands in the bushes a good fifteen feet from me. It is the most beautiful throw I have ever seen.

It is a year later. My son is playing on his third Little League team. He eats, sleeps, and breathes baseball. The adage, "Be careful what you wish for," comes to mind. He has become a TIVO expert, lining up more games to watch than his one-hour-per-day TV limit could ever allow him to view. He knows players, statistics, team records. And since his favorite player, Shawn Green, was traded, he's started to delve into the finer points of free agency.

Last month, I watched him in a game and noticed that he wasn't doing nearly as well fielding grounders as when I'd practiced with him. So, later, I took him out to a field and started hitting him ground balls with a bat, instead of throwing them to him on the concrete in front of our house like we usually do.

He was doing pretty well, so I started hitting the ball a bit harder. Then, a ground ball took a bad hop and smashed right into his nose. Hard.

My son has always been a big bleeder. This was no exception. Blood flowed like a river from his nose. I had to take off my shirt to collect it, feeling as low as a person could feel. He didn't exactly make me feel better.

"You hit it too hard, Daddy. You hurt me. Why did you hurt me?"

He bled for a good five minutes. Then we just lay on the grass in silence. Both of us traumatized. We looked up at the sky, lost in our own thoughts. My father hit me with a ball in the nose once too. We didn't use T-balls then either. My father insisted on official National League hardballs. I can feel the sting like it was yesterday. "Nice catch," was his only response. Then, I was expected to get right back out there and try again.

When I thought enough time had passed, I tried to explain to my son what had happened, that I hadn't intentionally thrown the ball at his nose, that I hadn't meant to hurt him. I only wanted to help him improve his baseball playing. If he was going to improve, he needed to learn how to field grounders from a batted ball on grass. A ball comes off a bat differently from when it is thrown, and the bounce is different on grass than on concrete. And sometimes you get bad hops. I explained to him that I was hitting him ground balls on grass to try to make him a better ballplayer.

He was silent for a long time. Then he rose.

He looked at me, his face stained with dried blood. "Let's play, Daddy," he said. He put on his glove and walked back out onto the field.

I started throwing him ground balls.

"No. With a bat," he said.

I picked up the bat and began to gingerly hit some slow grounders.

"Hit it harder, Daddy," he said. "Hit it as hard as you can."

I picked up the speed a little. And as I hit him grounders, hoping to hell he didn't get another bad hop, I thought about my son. About his tenacious-ness. His resolve. I thought about how hard he has had to work in his life to do simple things. Speak. Write. Perform basic coordinated movements. Have a conversation.

I thought about how much I admired him. I thought about the miracle of what was happening in front of my eyes. He figured out a way to do what his body never intended for him to do. To catch a ball, throw it, hit. Play baseball. We were doing the impossible. I was playing baseball on an open field with my son.

Then, as my son would say, "I got a smell." The grass had been cut recently. The scent permeated everything, bringing me back to a place and time long ago—playing baseball with my father at the pray grounds. I've never smelled anything sweeter.

Jason Katims

Leaving Literalville

Literalville is what I like to call the place where my son, Ramon, and other people with autism often reside, that place where everything is black and white. Facts and data don't change, and so can be trusted and memorized, unlike abstract or ambiguous concepts that you can't touch or picture. Anyone who spends time with someone with autism soon discovers the interesting issues that can result from strictly literal thinking. Visitors to our home who have shown up at 6:01 instead of the appointed 6:00 can tell you how Ramon accosts them, hollering, "You're late!" Repeated explanations of how we allow for a few minutes here and there fall on deaf ears. Other examples from Literalville are quite funny, including one time recently while we were taking a walk, and Ramon, now fourteen, complained to me that holding his water bottle was making his hand too cold. When I suggested he "hold the bottle higher" (meaning, where there was no liquid to make it cooler), he, of course, lifted it up over his head.

Ordinary figures of speech throw Ramon for a loop until he is told what they mean.

"No," I'll explain, "I don't mean you're really making me drive the car up the wall. I just mean you're making me very frustrated."

"Ohhh!" Ramon will say, and then we both laugh as we picture the car hanging sideways on the living room wall. Ramon's being grounded in the literal has helped us both to develop a pretty good sense of humor.

On rare occasions, though, Ramon, like many other people with autism, will leap from Literalville to the Land of Abstraction, and each time I am stunned by how much he can grasp. I have witnessed him pondering such intense concepts as God and death with the poignant thirst for understanding of any child. One such incident occurred two years ago, just days before Ramon's father was going to marry his step-mother.

Most people with autism also have a particularly hard time with big changes, and Ramon is no different. His hardest time is the few weeks leading up to the change, when he is uncertain as to how things will be. Once he sees the new house, new car, new school, or new schedule, he is happy to investigate it. I suppose this is natural, in some ways, to everybody. How many of us feel a similar anxiety when faced with something new? The main difference is that people with autism usually have a very difficult time articulating their fears, since even talking about what they fear creates anxiety.

When Ramon's dad and I divorced a few years back, Ramon had some acting-out behaviors at school for a few weeks during the time we were preparing the house for sale, which is nothing out of the ordinary for any child of eight. But the divorce was amicable, and he saw how his father and I continued to communicate almost daily. Since we were both cheerful and excited about the changes, he became happy too. Once Ramon saw that all the divorce meant for him was that he would spend time with Mom and Dad separately, in two different houses, he relaxed into the new routine and enjoyed the changes the new situation brought. Two bedrooms! Two TVs and VCRs! Two different kitchens containing different kinds of snacks!

In the weeks leading up to his dad's wedding, however, Ramon again began showing signs of anxiety. His defiance at home and at school escalated. He started crying at trivial things, sobbing inconsolably. His need to control his world became intense, and he even began to talk in his sleep. My ex and I talked about these behaviors, and we talked to Ramon's teacher. We finally chalked it up to twelve-year-old hormones or the coming summer break and waited for it to blow over.

None of us imagined that his behaviors had anything to do with the wedding, since it wasn't going to change anything concrete in Ramon's life. We were sure he understood that. I soon realized, though, that it wasn't the concrete things that Ramon was afraid of. It was the whole abstract notion of marriage, and how a new marriage might threaten to take someone's love away.

My ex and I had talked over the details with Ramon many times, stressing that nothing about his routine would change after the wedding. Lisa would become Ramon's step-mom, and her kids would become his step-siblings, and Ramon would still stay with them part of each week, like always. The wedding was to be small and on a weekday, and I assured Ramon I would pick him up from school and take him to it. We talked about the wedding ceremony, too, including who would be there and what Dad and Lisa would say and do. Since Lisa and I get along well and since my ex and I have maintained a respectful friendship, we thought our calmness and happiness about the coming nuptials would be enough to keep Ramon pacified. Of course, it wasn't that simple.

One night two weeks before the wedding, I noticed Ramon was particularly quiet and thoughtful. He got into his pajamas and brushed his teeth without his usual chatter of mimicking commercials or telling me his latest "crazy way" of getting from our house to Grandma's. He climbed into bed, and like every other night, I turned out the light and lay down next to him for a few minutes as he drifted off to sleep. Every so often, my being there during those last few minutes of his day has proven invaluable—like the time he told me about his fourth grade teacher physically abusing him or when he wanted to talk about his dog dying. This night proved to be such a night.

"Mom?" he asked. "Why is Dad marrying Lisa?"

Oh boy. A why question. One that broached the Land of Abstraction. I chose my words carefully.

"Well, because they love each other. They want to be a part of each other's families."

"Why can't Dad still be married to you?"

Wow. We had been divorced for over four years; I had no idea this thought ever entered Ramon's mind. It's such a normal thought for a child of divorce to have; why did I think my child wouldn't consider it just because he has autism? I tried to keep my answer clear and literal, to ensure it made sense to him.

"You know, your dad and I were married for a long time, thirteen years. We loved each other very much for the first part of that time. But then we decided that our love had changed, so it was time to stop being married and live in different places. Now, your dad loves Lisa. That doesn't mean he doesn't still love me, too; but it's a different kind of love. Did you know there are lots of kinds of love?"

"No."

"Think about all the people and places and things you love. You love your Nintendo games, right? And books. Do you think you love them the same way you love me?"

A pause. "No."

"See? And how about the way we love our pets. Do you love them the same way you love Dad and me?"

"No!"

"And what about Aunt Jan, or Grandma and Grandpa, or your cousins?"

"No, I love you the best."

"And moms and dads love their children the best of all, too. That's a special kind of love, and it's the most important. I love you, and Dad loves you, and that kind of love can never, ever change or go away. Okay?"

"Okay."

"But sometimes the kind of love a mom and dad have for each other can change. Dad and I still care a lot about each other, but we realized a few years ago that we didn't enjoy living in the same house together. Our love was more like a friendly love instead of a married people love. We still see each other all the time, don't we? We're still a part of your family. And we both still love you more than any-thing or anyone in the world."

I gave him a big, long hug, and he squeezed back harder than usual.

"But now Dad wants to marry Lisa? Because he loves her?" Ramon asked.

"Right. They love each other, and they want to make their two families into one big family. That's okay, isn't it? For you to have two moms and a new brother and sisters?"

"A mom and a step-mom," Ramon corrected me.

"You're right. I'll always be your mom. You came out of my tummy. But when you're at Dad's, Lisa can be a kind of mom too. She loves you very much, too, and it's okay for you to love her back. We can love lots of different people, in lots of different ways."

We were quiet for a while, as he sorted all these ideas.

Then he asked, "Can I get married too?"

I smiled. How normal a question can you get? "Sure, after you're all grown up."

"Can I marry you, Mom?"

(Didn't Freud write something about this?) "No, you can't marry someone that's already in your family. Remember, the whole reason you marry someone is to make them a part of your family. You might meet a nice lady one day when you're a grown-up, and decide you love her and want to make her a part of your family."

"Ohhh!" he said, in a long, drawn-out way that assured me he really understood.

"Ramon," I said in my most calm, most serious voice, holding his hand very tightly. "Your dad and

Lisa getting married doesn't change anything at all for us. You're just getting a bigger family, that's all. You'll have more people to love you and help take care of you. Won't that be great?"

"And a step-brother and two stepsisters!" he cried in his old excited voice.

"Yes! Isn't that awesome?"

He hugged me again, squeezing hard.

"I sure love you, Mom, so much."

"And I love you too, buddy. I always, always will. And so will Dad. We both love you most of all."

As he drifted off to sleep, I lay there several more minutes and let the weight of the experience sink in. What was autistic about the conversation he and I had just had? He had sensed there was more to this marriage thing than he understood, and he needed my reassurance that it wasn't going to alter anything that was most important in his life, not just his routine or where he slept each night, but the love and the family-ness too.

Ramon may live a great majority of the time in Literalville, but he's just like every other human when it comes to needing to understand such abstractions as love, family, and security. Sometimes, he's pretty good at talking about them too. I just need to be there to listen.

Kathryn Hutchinson

 Entomology

I always check the two cocoons hanging from the kitchen window above the sink right after breakfast. Yesterday, I noticed that they had turned from opalescent green and gold to translucent. Today, I could see the butterflies sleeping inside, ready to hatch. Each year my brother-in-law gives us two cocoons, and every year the two butterflies hatch at the same time, as though a secret signal has passed between them.

This year, I decide to wait until later, after I've tackled the breakfast dishes, to mention the impending hatching to the boys.

I thread my way through the path of LEGOs that snake around the kitchen table. The design, so careful and elaborate, is undoubtedly six-year-old Thomas's work. It certainly doesn't have the aura of catastrophe that marks the creations of three-year-old Patrick.

"Be careful," Thomas says without looking up. "Don't ruin my Alpha Force lab. And those are the obstacles."

Obstacles, indeed. "Can I clear a little spot so I can load the dishwasher?" I ask, wasting good sarcasm on Thomas.

He looks up, considers me for a moment. "Okay," he agrees, "But don't wreck anything."

I nudge a tower-like structure out of the way with my foot. "I'll try."

At least he is engrossed in the structural aspects of the Alpha Force lab. Usually, he runs a technical commentary for my benefit. As I clear the counter of breakfast dishes, I think about butterflies and their secret signals to each other.

Patrick races into the kitchen, pauses when he spots the enticing layout before him, and spontaneously launches himself at the closest structure. As Thomas shrieks, I catch Patrick with both hands and lift him clear of the wreckage. Patrick kicks his feet comically, as if he is still running, and squinches his face into a mixture of outrage and amusement. He knows he's funny; he cracks himself up all the time. And his facial expressions are indescribable. Until we knew that his brother, Thomas, had Asperger's syndrome, my husband and I were worried something was wrong with Patrick. He contorted his face endlessly, expressing constantly shifting emotions.

Thomas usually had the same expression, something like a slightly worried concentration, broken only occasionally by smiles of happiness or frowns of distress. Patrick, on the other hand, was the man with a thousand faces.

"Mom, he broke my retaining wall!" Thomas howls.

I set Patrick on a chair with a juice box to keep him busy. Certainly, all the best parenting books recommend distracting your children with high-calorie juice when necessary.

"I'll help you fix it," I offer Thomas.

Miraculously, he stops his sobs. We put the wall back together.

"Did you know my Alpha Force driver has to have the mechanic fix his vehicle?" Thomas asks.

"No, I did not," I say, snapping the last LEGO in place.

"See, this vehicle is the Tundra Tracker. It's designed for highly treacherous conditions. Only this driver can handle it. Did you know that the other vehicles are unable to handle the icy conditions . . . ?"

I turn back to loading the dishwasher, murmuring the occasional "uh-huh" as Thomas continues to explain his LEGO world to me. I've heard a lot of it already; the Alpha Force characters have been Thomas's passion for the past few months. Unbelievably, our local library even had books about LEGOs, which Thomas checked out over and over.

Patrick finishes his juice and jumps off the chair, fortunately missing the Ice Lab but slipping on a stray LEGO and falling to the floor with cries of pain. He's a tough kid; I could tell he was really hurt. I sit on the floor and pull him into my lap. He presses his face against me and cries in mingled pain and outrage. I try to look at his ankle where a small spot of blood wells, but he jerks his leg away.

Thomas came over and continued his lecture on the properties of ice that the Tundra Tracker might encounter.

"Thomas, Patrick is injured," I say above Patrick's crying and Thomas's monologue.

Thomas continues as though I hadn't spoken, his grey eyes slightly unfocused, looking at a spot just above and slightly behind me.

"The Alpha Force drivers can engage Alpha mode if necessary," he goes on.

"Thomas!" I yell.

He keeps talking, raising his voice a little to be heard above Patrick's cries.

What had all those books on Asperger's said about this situation? They never seemed to have the right examples. What was I supposed to do? Probably not just keep raising my voice.

"Thomas, come and look at the blood."

That gets his attention, and Patrick's wails quiet too.

"What?" Thomas asks, his eyes focusing on me.

"Patrick is bleeding. Come look."

Thomas sets down the Tundra Tracker and crouches in front of Patrick. A trickle of blood runs down my three-year-old's ankle. When I dab it with a paper napkin Patrick tenses but doesn't say anything. Thomas leans in and peers closely at the wound.

"I think I can see your muscle. And your bone," he says solemnly.

Excellent bedside manner from the budding physician. Maybe he could be a surgeon and not talk to the patients. However, his technique charms his brother.

"Yeah, my bone," Patrick says, his tears gone. "I need a Band-Aid."

"I'll get you one," Thomas says and hops up.

I sit holding Patrick, incredulous. My God, Thomas is being helpful. Compassionate, even.

Thomas returns with the bandage and peels off the wrapper. He positions the Band-Aid precisely over the wound and smoothes it onto his brother's ankle.

"Is Thomas a doctor?" Patrick asks.

"He is today," I say.

"There, Patrick," Thomas says in his careful, precise tone. "The Band-Aid will heal it."

"Thank you, Thomas," I say. "You were very helpful to your brother."

I give myself an imaginary gold star for commenting on good behavior in Thomas. Positive reinforcement. Maybe that will cancel out my yelling at him earlier.

Thomas acts as if he hasn't heard me. "Look," he says, pointing to the window above the kitchen sink.

I follow his gaze to the butterfly cocoons. Both of the butterflies have emerged. One still clings to the remnants of the cocoon, and the other is perched on the window screen, slowly opening and closing its wings.

"They're beautiful," Thomas says softly.

I turn to look at him, at his rapt expression.

I pull over a chair so Patrick can climb up on it and see the butterflies too. The three of us watch them silently for a little while. The late morning sunshine makes the Monarchs' wings look like molten jewels.

"Can we keep them as pets?" Thomas asks.

He always wants more pets, as long as they are insects, reptiles, or birds. He isn't wild about mammals, though. In fact, when my old dog died at age fourteen, Thomas pondered the situation for a moment and then said he was glad she was dead.

"She ate my waffles," he said, frowning with the painful memory.

"When I grow up, there will be no dogs in my house," Thomas declared another time.

I tried not to take it personally. It's okay to dislike dogs, I guessed.

"No, we can't keep the butterflies in the house," I say. "They are wild creatures, and they can live in our flower bed."

"But I could keep them in my room and bring them flowers every day!" Thomas says, his voice rising.

"No, honey." Quick, another topic to distract him. "Let's look up butterflies while we wait for their wings to dry off. Go find the bug book."

Patrick shoves at Thomas to seize the bug book first, but at least the skirmish doesn't escalate. I find the page on monarchs, and we sit on the floor with the book in my lap, a little boy on each side of me.

"*Danaus plexippus*," I say, reading the scientific name.

Thomas pronounces it after me, sounding as if he loves the very syllables in the word. I know how he feels. Maybe I shouldn't do that. Am I just setting him up for ridicule? He'll be the first grader who knows the Latin names for all the common butterflies. He won't forget, and some day it will come up in casual conversation—or in a lecture to his classmates, anyway. But I love the way he loves to learn.

"Chrysalis is another word for cocoon," I read. "It comes from the Greek word for golden." It is fascinating.

"I wonder why the butterflies always hatch at the same time," I say, and pull another book off the shelf. I thumb through the encyclopedia and tell the boys about monarch butterfly migration. They look interested for a while but then turn back to the bug book.

"Where's the picture of the leeches?" Thomas asks.

I help him find the page with the bloodsuckers, his favorite page.

"Worms," Patrick says.

"No, Patrick, not worms. Leeches," Thomas explains. "They suck your blood. But this kind only sucks fish blood . . . Mom, can I get a pet leech?" Thomas asks.

"I'll call the pet store and ask if they have any," I say absently. Then I think, *Wait, should I say things like that? Maybe I should reread some of the autism books.*

Thomas stands up and drapes his arms around my neck. It takes me a moment to realize he is hugging me. His hugs are a little awkward, unskilled, and if you give him a kiss, he seems to like it but always wipes it off with his hand. I hug him back.

"Mom, I love butterflies," he says, his eyes fixed on the middle distance. "And leeches."

"Me too," I say.

He lets go of me and walks back to the kitchen window to check on the butterflies.

Maybe he would grow up to be a great butterfly expert. Or a leech expert, with only invertebrates and no dogs in his house. I hope he has people in his house, people who love him as I do and who will know he wasn't trying to be cruel when he said he was glad that my dog was dead. People who will know what it is like to have a subject, like butterflies or Alpha Force LEGOs, capture your whole heart and soul, and give your life meaning.

I hear Thomas talking to the butterflies while I put away the books.

"Good bye, *Danaus plexippus*. We'll never forget you. Good luck with your migration." He pauses. "Would you like to see my Tundra Tracker before you go?"

Angie Lathrop

The Head in the Head

Our son, Henry, was given an interchangeable diagnosis of Asperger's syndrome and high-functioning autism when he was three. Although learning of the diagnosis was difficult, it provided answers and hope. We read everything we could find, made appointments with speech pathologists, occupational therapists, and psychologists, and continued our appointments at a clinic for autism. It has all been helpful.

There was only one area that no amount of therapy seemed to help—our son's anxiety. When he felt safe, he was the happiest little boy in the world and able to engage in life, love, and learning. But many things made him nervous, and I couldn't figure out how to prevent and alleviate his anxiety. Why did he panic and cry when I left the room? Why was it virtually impossible for him to feel safe unless I was within 2 feet of him?

It is heartbreaking to see your child suffer. The worst part was hearing other mothers talk of their neuro-typical children and how they were able to help them overcome separation anxiety. I felt so alienated; I knew they didn't understand. Most of them recommended "tough love." Against my instincts, I tried it a couple of times, leaving him with his grandma or a close friend. Disastrous. He'd break into hives and cry uncontrollably, and I would be left questioning my parental abilities and consumed with regret. He couldn't navigate through anything without me, and while that was okay with me, it is not okay in life. I wanted him to know he could safely go to school, play at a friend's house, or visit his grandma.

The psychologist suggested medication. Psychotropics on a four-year-old? I was overwhelmed. We tried some alternatives first—yoga, more therapy, swimming, and lots of prayers on my part. Then, eventually, he began to acquire some new experiences with my being 10 feet away, then 20, and then all on his own with his grandma or aunt.

We started special education public preschool, and his individualized education plan (IEP) provided extra therapies. Reluctantly, Henry gave it a try, provided I was waiting for him afterward in the same spot in front of the school, at the same time, everyday. He was also able to attend Sunday school. It was a great year. Just as I'd hoped, he was developing his own sense of who he was and what he could do—and he could do so much. His confidence grew. I was so proud of him. It was time for kindergarten.

As usual, it was a difficult start, especially after having the summer off, but we had some great transitional tools. His reading was now at about a third-grade level, so it was very helpful for him to carry a schedule in his hands. He would hold it tightly, consulting it at the first sign of anxiety. As anyone close to a person with Asperger's knows, information is enormously comforting. It is a factual, dependable, and trustworthy anchor in a world that is often too unpredictable to kids like Henry.

His teacher was a blessing. The principal was so supportive. We all worked together. Within a month of rough mornings, Henry was able to say goodbye to me with confidence. He loved learning, playing, and making friends. The teachers in the mainstream classes often invited Henry to come read to their students. The second and third graders marveled at the abilities of this little kindergartner, and Henry beamed.

Pretty soon he was leaving the classroom on his own to use the bathroom (a big deal), eating lunch without his teacher nearby (another big deal), and basically owning every inch of that campus. Due to his unbelievable ability to memorize, he knew the number of each classroom and the teacher in it, the

school schedule, and the location of just about everything. He felt safe, right at home. He loved visiting
the principal. All our hard work had paid off. We
were so proud of him, and we looked forward to first
grade, where he would likely be mainstreamed, with
some extra-curricular therapy.

Then one day about eight months into his
kindergarten year as we were driving to school, he
didn't want to go. We talked about how sometimes
you might lose interest in something, but when you
go and try, you start to enjoy it again. He was skep-
tical, but he went. The next day he was even more
hesitant. The next day he was holding back tears.
We tried talking it out at home. What was bothering
him? He didn't know. Had something happened to
scare him? A teacher? A classmate? No. What was it?
Why this sudden change? I took him to school every
day for two weeks, and every day he came right back
home in tears. I started to lose my patience. I was
doing everything I knew to do, but we were getting
nowhere. Then came day fourteen of his refusal to
go to school.

We walked slowly to the classroom. I could tell
immediately he was not going to be able to do it. The
tears started, and the panic and hives. Exasperated, I
dropped to my knees outside the classroom.

"Henry," I whispered as I held him. "Please let me
help you. I am not angry or disappointed. I am here

to help you, but I can't if you cannot tell me what has happened. We have been coming to school for almost two years now. You have really come to love it here. You have nice friends and a terrific teacher. I know how much you love to visit the principal. I am so proud of you for all the work you've done. I don't want you to lose something you enjoy. Please, honey, talk to me. Use your words. I know it's hard. Please try."

"Mommy," he said, tears streaming down his face, "There is a head in my head. It floats around and tells me I can't do things. Mommy, you are right about school. I do love it here."

He struggled with his words, and as he became more desperate, his voice got louder. "I have come here over and over again. I have good friends here. I love my teacher and my principal. I know I am safe here, but there is this head in my head. I know I can do it. I want to do it, but I can't."

His voice got even louder, his eyes continued to swell, and hives covered his face and neck. "The head says I can't, even though I want to. That head in my head! I just want it out! Out! Out!" he screamed as he hit his forehead with his fist repeatedly.

He curled up on top of me, sobbing. I wept for him. His teacher and the principal stood and watched with tears in their eyes as I lifted Henry up off the floor and carried him to the car, my heart aching with his.

I called the clinic. We started an antidepressant and cognitive therapy. Initially, there was no change. Henry was back where he'd been at the beginning. He panicked when I left the room; he could no longer play next door or stay with Grandma. He and I were secluded at home, struggling to regain all he'd lost.

One month later, he was still unable to attend school. At his annual IEP meeting, the teacher and principal had no choice but to suggest we transfer to a special education campus, in the event his debilitating anxiety continued into the next school year. I knew this suggestion was merely a hopeless formality. They didn't have the resources to help him, and neither would any other public school.

I looked into private schools for autism, but they were too expensive. I decided to home-school in the fall if he were still struggling. While home-schooling is a viable solution for children with Asperger's who don't enjoy socializing, my son is the opposite. Contrary to the stereotype, he is outgoing, has a warm personality, and loves to be around people. It would be a shame to keep him hidden away, all for the "head in the head."

By the last week of school, the medication and therapy began to take the edge off his anxiety, and he was able to finish kindergarten. I am certain these therapies were invaluable in his returning to school, but I know they were not entirely responsible. I know this because Henry is no longer on medication and currently does not need a therapist, and he is having a terrific year. So what is this all about?

It's about the head in the head. As frightening as that experience was, it revealed to me the very essence of one's struggle with autism. Those of us outside the spectrum have fears and anxieties too, but the head in our heads is quieted by our intuition, our innate sense of well being, and our predisposition to know things will probably be okay. People with autism are far less intuitive. Instead, they rely on more tangible things—like calendars, schedules, rules, teachers one learns to trust, and most of all, mothers and fathers—to quiet their fears. Yet, none of these things can completely quell the head in the head of a person with autism. Occasionally, the head wins, and the person retreats.

I believe this need to retreat is more "normal" than those of us without autism realize, and is only exaggerated by the condition. We live in a world that is not structured for our beautiful, eccentric, gifted, and unique children; it is structured for those of us with the neurobiological ability to make sense of cues from the world around us. The head in Henry's head is a persistent daily challenge that I now greatly respect. Because of it, he needs more time to himself than the average person. Time when the head in the head is quiet. Time to just be. We all need this time, but the person with Asperger's needs it more. It is crucial.

The head in the head is not the enemy; it is only a reminder that our little ones are the bravest people on the planet. They courageously step into the world each day without a road map, and they try. This realization has been a huge source of comfort to me and helped me to better understand and help my son.

I worry less now. I know not to take anything for granted. Perhaps that's one of the blessings wrapped up in the sometimes difficult world of autism. We parents know how to celebrate the good times, and we also know they don't always last. The head in the head has taught me not to judge and to go with the ebb and flow of my son's sense of himself and the world as he experiences it. It has shown me that he is much more than a child on the spectrum of autism. He is a whole human being whose wiring and inner world are unique to him—an extraordinary person in an ordinary world.

I no longer limit my expectations for him or try to conform to some formula of "normalcy." I now have only acceptance for the amazing person he is and hope that my child, who struggles enough, will find a refuge in his life with me, his sister, and his dad. And I hope he will always know that there is no school year or play date or task that is more important than his feelings. His internal gauge is more accurate than any other.

This to me is Asperger's: the constant balance of getting out into the world and yet accepting and respecting the unique beauty of the condition. It has its own rules, and most of them are different from ours. It demands that parents throw away convention and think outside the box. I have come to embrace and enjoy this world, and to appreciate the head in my head. The one that tells me to stop, let go, be still for a while, and then try again.

Shawn Daywalt Lutz

To Welcome Chance

On the day his son was born, Andy launched a thousand blue and white balloons.

He was with the outside broadcast unit of the radio station where we both worked at the time. The station sponsors the city junior athletic championships, and when the competitions are over we let off balloons stamped with our logo and contact details. Sometimes people call from hundreds of miles away in Scotland or across the English Channel. That year, Andy decided to write his son's name on some of the balloons. He wanted everyone to know Joe Donnelly had come into the world.

The first one gets you like that. Andy was so excited he'd rushed straight from the maternity hospital to the sports field, his feet scarcely touching the ground. I was an old hand by then. I'd had five babies, though I tried not to mention this too often. It rarely failed to provoke the question, "How on earth do you manage?" (And that's before I tell them Alice, my youngest, is autistic with severe learning difficulties—and no, she hasn't any special skills.)

Andy knew very little about my domestic circumstances. I was only a freelancer on the arts program, dropping into the station occasionally to deliver a piece or edit an interview. The Andy Donnelly Show was one of the most popular. He had loads of fan mail, mostly from pensioners and schoolgirls, who'd been heartbroken when he married Kat. They were like chalk and cheese, the two of them: she, tall, grave, and serene; Andy, gregarious and bursting with affability.

I sent a blue romper suit as a present for the baby, but I didn't actually see little Joe until he was a year old, when the athletic championships came round again. I'd come to the event because one of my sons was competing. I had to make the most of my Alice-free hours, because once she came home, all my time was absorbed in looking after her. I stood by the line and cheered, and noticed Kat with a buggy a few yards away and the child sitting immobile, like a small, inscrutable Buddha. I watched Andy come over and try to curl his son's fingers around a bunch of balloon strings, but Joe ignored his attempts and all the balloons with his name on them floated free.

Some months later, Andy ran straight into me in the station's sound-proofed corridor. Normally, he was always so relentlessly social, he'd never walk past without a greeting, but I might as well have been a piece of wall. He had a habit of biting his lip when he was worried (which wasn't very often), and I noticed flecks of blood on his chin.

I apologized for the collision and then asked, "Are you okay?"

He shook his shaggy mop of hair as if he were trying to clear his head. He began to mutter, "Yeah . . . fine . . ." Then he stopped and looked at me as though remembering I was the one who had all the kids.

"Joe had his eighteen-month assessment yesterday," he said.

I nodded. This was familiar territory, but I didn't want to pre-empt anything.

"He didn't do too well. They think he might be deaf."

I could see from the horror on his face that this was his worst nightmare. Andy lived for music. His own CD collection was as extensive as the station's. He played guitar and keyboard, he whistled on the street; no doubt he sang in the shower. He couldn't bring himself to imagine a world of silence.

"Of course," he went on, "It might just be glue-ear. They're going to run some tests."

"I'm sure he'll be okay," I said soothingly. You can't help it—it's human nature to reassure, even when something in the pit of your stomach or the deepest recesses of your brain is saying, *I wonder if . . .*

Most parents of disabled children find out there's something wrong soon after the birth. One unsettling aspect of autism is that it can take so long to identify; there's so much variation along the spectrum, so much scope for misinterpreting the signs. And the cases that get written up tend to be the unusual ones that interest the investigators, not the ones like my dear, sweet, low-achieving Alice.

She had actually passed both her early assessments. She was so responsive then, she fooled everybody. She loved attention and was disarmingly affectionate in return. She was a placid, gurgling, happy child who'd seemed as normal (if less troublesome) than her brothers and sisters—until the cracks began to show. Her speech faltered and disappeared; her restlessness increased; she seemed incapable of following instructions. She couldn't play; she could only watch TV. Eventually, I realized that if she couldn't adjust herself to our world, it was up to us to be creative and adjust ourselves to hers. People constantly remarked on the devotion and tenderness of her siblings, the way they took care of her. They knew the joys of unconditional love.

Andy and Kat had no other children to compare with Joe, so how could they tell which aspects of his behavior were normal and which bizarre?

It was close to two years after that chance encounter with Andy that I got a call right out of the blue.

"Hi, this is Kat Donnelly."

"Oh, Kat!" I said, surprised. We'd met a few times at work functions, but I hardly knew her. "How are you?"

"I hope you don't mind me asking, but someone told me you have an autistic daughter?"

"Yes, I do." I'm not ashamed of Alice. Actually I'm proud of her. Nobody who meets her fails to be enchanted by her stunning looks and her infectious laughter. I have to keep the meetings short, though. She can't stay in one place for any length of time; she's always on the move. Of course, it isn't easy, she isn't easy—in fact, she's exhausting. But our lives are never dull.

"I'm sorry, I only just found out."

"There's no reason why you should know. I don't broadcast it."

"No." She paused. "Well, I was wondering if I could talk with you." Her light, agitated voice came in a rush over the phone line. "You see, I had a feeling right from the beginning there was something odd about Joe. He was too quiet, you know? Andy said he took after me, but it was more than that. Then, they wondered if he might be deaf."

"Yes, I heard."

"And Andy was, like, so devastated. But now . . ."

No one would wish autism on a person; no one would be pleased at the diagnosis. But when you come across someone else who is affected by the condition, you welcome the sense of relief that, after all, you are not alone. Someone else is going through what you're going through, and there is comfort in that shared experience.

We agreed to meet for a coffee. When we met, Kat's makeup was flawless, but I could see through it to the lines of distress, the tremor in her hand as she lifted her cup. Joe was almost four. His private nursery school had been concerned about his behavior—he'd sit in a corner with a blanket over his head for hours—and Kat and Andy had been taking him to pediatric specialists.

"But they're so vague. They mutter about global developmental delay and say they don't like giving labels."

"Tell me about it!"

"The thing is, Andy won't accept there's anything wrong."

"And you reckon there is?"

"I wish I didn't, but I've been doing a lot of reading and so on. That's why I wanted to hear about Alice."

We talked for hours, often going over the same ground. I could see Kat trying to suppress shivers of recognition, shudders of concern.

"I don't suppose it's much consolation," I said. "But it does get easier as they get older. Alice generally sleeps through the night now; she's dry too."

"I don't know how you can be so . . . calm about it all."

"Well, I don't waste time blaming myself or thinking 'if only.' And I'm lucky enough to have other kids who are great at helping out.

"Two things in particular come to mind," I went on. "One, there's always someone worse off than you are, and two, the human spirit has an amazing ability to cope. But you have to start by accepting the way things are."

"The trouble is, Andy keeps making excuses for Joe. He won't believe me."

I nodded. Poor Andy. He made his living talking, charming thousands of unseen listeners. How could he countenance a child who might never say a word, might never connect? That must be as terrifying a prospect for him as deafness.

"My husband had difficulty accepting it, too," I said. "Everyone does. You keep thinking there must be some other explanation for the behavior. Then you start looking for a miracle cure."

"I don't believe in miracles," said Kat.

She pushed back her chair abruptly and fumbled for change for the coffee. Then she sighed. "He wants us to go to the athletics event again. Send off some more balloons with Joe's name on them."

"Well, it doesn't do any harm does it? Treating him like a normal child as far as you can."

Not long after that conversation, I was passing through the newsroom while Andy's show was being broadcast. His producer was putting through a call from Ireland.

"Hullo there?" I heard Andy say. "Can you give us your name and where you're from?"

The line crackled, and then abruptly cleared. "Well, now," creaked a man who sounded about ninety. "You wouldn't have heard of my village, I don't suppose, but we're in County Cork."

"And you say you've found one of our balloons?"

"I have so."

"Brilliant! That's fantastic news, you know, because it's so rare for any of them to fetch up west-wards. The prevailing winds nearly always blow them towards the continent. You're a lucky man . . . what did you say your name was?"

"Joe. Joe Donnelly."

Everyone in the newsroom stopped what they were doing and stared up at the speakers. For nearly half a minute, Andy was silent in shock.

"Joe Donnelly?"

"That's right. Sure, wasn't it a grand surprise for me when I came across one of them balloons with my very own name on it."

"It's m-my s-son's too," I'd never heard Andy stutter before.

"Well, would you listen to that!" The old man's soft lilting voice, as astonished as we all were, breezed over the airwaves. "And he's a grand little chap I'll be bound. How old is he now?"

"He's just turned four."

"And does he give you a moment's peace with his chatter there?"

I felt myself stiffen on Andy's behalf, as he steeled himself to answer. "Actually, he doesn't speak. He's, um, what's called autistic."

Silently, we all applauded him. His mailbag was going to be enormous.

"Then, God love us, it's a true miracle," said old Joe Donnelly. "That your boy with no words in his head has sent a message all this way, and I have been the one to find it. A blessed miracle."

Well, everybody was talking about that call for days. There were all kinds of theories. But a miracle? I didn't think so. A wild coincidence, certainly. A crazy fluke. Or how about a random accident of life, like the condition of autism itself? As for me, I like to think of it as a lesson in learning to appreciate the unexpected, to welcome chance.

Penelope Feeny

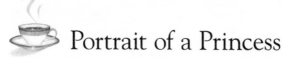

Portrait of a Princess

My daughter, Laurel, is a magical child. She comes from a land of unicorns and flying fish, dragons and manatees, woolly mammoths and willipedes. A land of blue foxes that live in igloos and snow white Lipizzaners who share castles with hedgehogs. In this land, worms have been known to find true love in a plate of spaghetti, and lemurs vote a straight party ticket. This is the place where Aunt Winnie, the Pegasus, takes high tea with General Washington; where mama wolverines rescue errant Redcoats from whitewater rapids; and where the Evil Mouse can dream up nothing that the Rescue Reindeer can't put right by supper.

Sadly, Laurel is forced to live in the real world. She's adapted, overall, as well as an Alien Princess can. She's mastered the skills of riding her training wheel bike and dawdling over chores, and she excels at popping her twin brother's fragile male ego with one withering insult. She shares . . . well, like any other seven-year-old. She manages to follow one-part directions with only the average amount of difficulty. She has a huge, if idiosyncratic, vocabulary; a strangely dry sense of humor; and a near-photographic memory for dialog. (This last, combined with a singing voice reminiscent of a tiny Ethel Merman, has resulted in more than one concert in the paper goods section of Wal-Mart: "Ev'ra-bodee! Ev'ra-bodee wants ta be a cat!")

Laurel reads at near-college level and has been doing so since kindergarten—a skill we discovered quite by accident, when she developed a literary taste ranging from obstetric nursing textbooks to Sharyn McCrumb's Ballad novels. I wasn't too clear, at the time, whether she understood what she was reading, but she cleared up that issue pretty quickly.

"Darlin', I don't know if that's a good choice to read," I said, indicating the paperback mystery novel she'd just picked up.

"Why?"

"Well, somebody dies."

"Oh." She considered this for a minute, and then asked, "Is it Elizabeth or Eileen?"

She finished the book that night.

There are conversational benefits to her wide-ranging tastes, of course. She'll hold forth at length on dinosaurs, skeletons, and weasels—and occasionally on more offbeat topics, like the poisonous qualities of oleander. She's a great friend in one-on-one situations, particularly if the friend likes books and horses better than Polly Pockets and Barbie. She adores art and draws wonderfully detailed and fantastical scenes from her home planet and, occasionally, the obstetric textbooks. She also adores crafts, singing, and drama, and has a not-so-secret ambition to beat her brother at Super Smash Brothers.

Laurel does have some challenges in her life, though. This world can be a pretty frightening place. It's populated by dogs, lobsters, motorcycles, and all manner of "Loud Scary Things." She's also not fond of baby dolls, particularly the ones with eyes that open and shut. In fact, real babies aren't among her favorites, either. She's convinced that they're out to attack her and take her toys, an opinion sadly reinforced by a few of the toddlers we've met at local play parks. As for bees and wasps . . . well, we won't go into detail, other than to suggest she's earned the right to be nicknamed "The Bee Banshee."

She's learned to handle her fears by telling a grownup (usually, but not exclusively, Mommy) and asking to hold hands until the Scary Thing goes away. But sometimes she forgets, and then she's been known to howl. Emphatically. Loudly. In fact, Jamie Lee Curtis would be in awe of this child.

What works best at this point is eye contact accompanied by a calm, firm "Laur, no screaming." I'd be lying if I didn't qualify this by saying that sometimes, at the end of a long day, my "Laur, no screaming" is phrased as "Knock it off."

The key is to get her to focus—and, if necessary, by making her look at your nose. A moment or two of focusing or counting freckles, and she's calm enough to continue with whatever activity the Scary Thing interrupted. (I'll also admit that I've wondered whether, when she's thirty, she'll still be calming herself by counting freckles or inspecting for boogers or whatever it is she does when she's staring at noses. But I suppose it's considerably less maladaptive than, say, baying like a deranged werewolf and aiming for a back-to-the-womb experience via the original cesarean site.)

Laurel's biggest challenge, however, has been in learning to "pass." Two years in the county public school system have demonstrated that our society has little patience with Alien Princesses. Bullies abound; parent volunteers shy away from little girls who are better read and more articulate than most of the PTA board; and not all "inclusion specialists" are conversant in the many things that go into the makeup of Princesses from her particular world.

So now she's learning a new skill. Camouflage.

As a native Floridian, she's familiar with the small lizards who overrun our yard, and she'll happily discuss in detail the precise shade of greeny brown they've turned in an effort to avoid standing out and thus becoming cat chow. The lesson appeals to her. She knows that standing out can be a problem for her, too, at times, and that there are advantages to developing her very own version of greeny brown. Perhaps, for example, it's not necessary to discuss the composition of baloney at the lunch table or to share everything she knows about pelvic ligaments with the substitute teacher. And it may be a good idea to list Franny K. Stein's *Lunch Walks Among Us* as her reading selection for this week's homework, rather than her original choice of *MacPherson's Lament*. Resisting the urge to micromanage play dates is harder, but she usually sees the value in trying and is fortunate to have one or two playmates who are willing to get beyond the occasional lapse.

Laurel knows she's not an average, ordinary little girl. Is she comfortable with it? Hard to say. She's never mentioned it herself. I suspect, from close observation, that she's at once fascinated and repelled by her older sister's charisma and the swarm of friends it attracts, and bewildered by her twin's ability to adapt to social situations in typical, easy, little-boy fashion.

For myself, I used to think occasionally—wistfully—of a cure for her form of autism. But in many ways her disability has brought to light other, greater abilities. And to hope for a cure for the simple fact of being Laurel has become unthinkable.

Jenan Gray

Cake and Polyester Don't Mix

Nick paced back and forth on the sidewalk. Across the street, white paper wedding bells hung on an iron post above the sign that read: Scott and Elizabeth's Wedding. The bells were silent, but Nick's mind was not: *Curses, how could she!* His fifteen-year-old brain circulated through every beloved cartoon movie he'd watched (over and over and over) that contained a wedding scene. He was trying to make sense of things. Cinderella got to marry her handsome prince. *Was Scott really Mom's Prince Charming or just some trickster, like Jafar in* Aladdin? Worst of all, this wedding meant change, big change. The world was always changing and that scared him so much.

In his hand he held the letter his mother had written him, now damp from his sweaty palms. He read it one more time.

Dear Nick,

This is a letter to talk about the wedding. Please read it. I know you are scared and unsure about all of this. It will be different for you to have a stepdad and stepbrothers. It will be new for a while, but I think you will like it. Remember, you don't have to give up your room!

Weddings are very special times. It is important to people that their family be there with them at the wedding. My family lives far away. Because they live far away, they can't be here at our wedding. You and your brother, Ben, are my family. I want you to be at the wedding very much. Our wedding won't be anything like a TV show or video.

Our wedding will be at the gazebo across the street. Our friends will be there, and they will want to talk to you and share this happy time. I will walk down the path, and I want you and Ben to be with me, arm-in-arm. Then you can sit down and just watch. It will be very quiet there. We will light candles. Some people will talk a little bit. Then when it's over, we will take pictures and go eat at a nice restaurant.

Mostly, I love you very much. I will be so happy to look at you when I am getting married and know that you love me enough to be there even if it scares you. Scott loves you too, and he wants you there too. Once we are married, we will all be a family. It will all be okay.

Love, Mom

Nick had changed his mind so many times in the last few days. Earlier that day, he had promised her he would go, and a part of him wanted to. Another part of him was just too scared. That made him angry. Soon, he didn't know what he felt. So much confusion! His mother tried to talk him into it. Earlier that week she'd bought him new shoes, new pants, a new belt, and even a tie. Today, he put on the clothes, but as the time of the wedding drew near, all he could say to her over and over was a line from the wedding scene in *The Little Mermaid*: "Don't you know cake and polyester don't mix!"

His mother finally gave up. She told him she would miss him, but that he could stay home if he really needed to. He had watched through the window as his mother took the arm of his brother, Ben, and headed down the gravel path to the gazebo in the neighbor's yard. They disappeared behind the thick laurel hedge, as tall as the briar bushes in *Sleeping Beauty*. Once everyone had left his house, he realized how lonely and quiet it was without them.

Now Nick paced back and forth on the sidewalk, careful to avoid the cracks. He wouldn't want his mother's back to break, especially at the wedding. He knew one thing: Even though Donald Duck had never married Daisy Duck and Mickey Mouse had never married Minnie Mouse, they really loved each other. He really loved his mom and wanted her to be happy.

He looked down at the frogs on his tie. His mom had bought him a silly tie with frogs on it and a new green shirt too. Nick loved frogs. They changed from tadpoles to pollywogs and finally to frogs. Maybe tadpoles were scared of change too, but somehow they managed to become frogs. Why couldn't he just hop across the street?

No, it was too wide. He had never crossed the street alone before. He'd always had someone with him. Now it was too late. Everyone was already across the street at the wedding. Still, he had practiced before, and after all, he was fifteen. It was time to learn how to be a man.

His heart was pounding. He looked both ways. There were no cars coming. He took a deep breath and stepped out into the street. He dashed across to the other side. He still gripped the letter in his hand. Now he carefully folded it and put it in his back pocket.

On the other side of the hedge, he could see the people gathered for the wedding. There were roses and candles, and he recognized everyone there. He had known most of them since he was a very little boy. He didn't feel as afraid as he did a minute ago, and he had proven himself brave and unselfish, like Pinocchio. He had kept his promise.

When he reached the gazebo, everyone turned to look at him. Scott smiled and waved. His mother was smiling too, but tears were spilling out of her eyes. He wasn't sure if this meant she was sad or happy, but he suddenly felt very warm inside and safe. He'd finally reached the shore after swimming in very deep water, like Piglet from *Winnie the Pooh* during the big flood.

Nick listened as everyone took turns saying things. He understood the words "love, family, togetherness." He rocked slightly back and forth, waiting patiently for his turn. Even though his words often didn't come out just right, he knew what he wanted to say. When it was his turn, he did:

"Mom, Scott, keep the faith. I love a miracle. Now you two can really get on to loving. After all, everyone just loves a happy ending."

Elizabeth King Gerlach

 Flying

I'm getting tired of vacuum cleaners, Jonah's second true love after water. His obsession with drains makes me a little uncomfortable (although, I reason with myself, maybe it will led to a water systems job); plus, they're boring. I decide it's time to further groom his interest in airplanes. So I drop him off at the gym with a helper. I have one hour.

There is a pilot supply store right next door to the gym, with an open door beneath a welcoming red windsock. I step inside, but I'm nervous. I have never asked for anything connected to Jonah's disability other than the home program of applied behavioral analysis, speech, and occupational therapies. I don't know what to expect.

The sunlit shop is large and crammed with accessories. Looking at the banners spanning the shop, I start to feel positive. I picture a small Disneyland of friendly pilots awaiting our plea, a flying corps of do-gooders on standby to help my child.

A slender woman with tart brown eyes steps in front of me. "Can I help you?" she asks. There is a tightness in her face that gives me pause.

"Is the owner around?" I ask.

"I can help you."

I remind myself that I am there for Jonah. "I have a son; he's three. He loves airplanes and—"

The phone rings. She holds a manicured-nailed finger up to me, steps behind the counter, and takes the call. Her impassive face becomes pleased, lively, and I think, *Yes, this might work.*

She hangs up. "Yes, you were saying?"

"Do you know any pilots?" I ask.

"Yes. Why?"

"I know it's a strange question, but my son is handicapped. He has a form of autism. He is so interested in airplanes, and they make him talk more. Would it be possible—"

"I'll be with you in a minute," she calls out to an older gentleman looking around the store. "And?" she says, looking back at me. Her mascara-heavy lashes are very black in the sunlight, like spiders.

"Well, if he could just sit inside a plane . . . it would be so good for him. Just once, to sit inside of a plane."

Her face freezes. "No way could I do that. I can't put myself in a position like that."

"Oh," I say.

"That's just too much."

"But you know pilots, right?" I ask, suddenly aware I am begging.

"Yes, I know pilots. We have hundreds of pilots. Jet pilots, commercial airlines," she says with pride, looking over my shoulder.

"Well, I want to find a pilot who would let him sit in a plane."

"No," she says. "I'm far too busy for that. You can't ask me to put myself in that position."

My face crumples and then hardens. I had called Jonah handicapped before her, given her our greatest need and confidence, and now I'm angry. She keeps talking after me as I head toward the door, and I wonder, *Did she misunderstand?*

"I'm not asking for a flight," I say. "Just for him to sit in a plane, on the ground."

"I'm way too busy for that. You can't ask me to do that."

"Yes," I say loudly. "Too busy."

Too busy to help a disabled child, I want to yell as I stand shaking on the sunny sidewalk outside. But I can't allow myself to give up. *Remember your childhood riding lessons,* I think. *This is just a horse that's bucked you off. Get up and get back on that horse.*

I drive through the surrounding streets to the small airport. As I head toward the main door of the flight school, I look in the glass at my reflection. A woman, her blond hair whipped by the morning breeze, with baggy jeans draping her legs underneath the practical coat. Something desperate about her.

A young man and a young woman in uniform sit behind the desk. "May I help you?" asks the girl.

I go into a scant explanation about Jonah, telling her he is a special-needs kid who talks about planes and needs to step inside of one. I say I live close by and that I can drive over at any pilot's convenience. The girl nods; the boy listens.

"We don't know of anyone like that off-hand, but there are some really sweet pilots that come in," she says. "I'll keep your number and ask around."

With tears falling, I return to the gym for Jonah and his helper. I sweep up my son and tell him, "Mommy's going to get you on a plane someday."

"See the airplane?" he calls in a high, excited note, pointing to a helicopter over our heads.

"Yes, baby, I see the airplane."

I feel sick the rest of the day about the woman at the supply store. I wonder whether she feels guilty, whether she repeated the conversation to a boyfriend or maybe a pilot. I wonder if she defended herself, and if her listener looked sideways at her with doubt in his heart. Then I realize that this is a fantasy and that I'll be happier if somehow I can think charitably of her.

Before noon the next day, a young pilot calls. He got our number from the flight school. "Would you and your son like to come do a check-out on a Cessna right now?"

My eyes dart to the clock. We have an hour before naptime. "Give me ten minutes," I tell him. "Jonah will be thrilled."

It's a wild, bright-blue day. Paul, the young pilot, hops in our car and directs me to drive along the wide, windy runway. Planes bump through the air overhead as they approach for landing. Through Jonah's open window, we can see smaller craft parked wingtip-to-wingtip, their blue, red, and green markings like the flags of small nations.

Paul leads us to his plane, a white one with green paint. Jonah's eyes are transfixed.

"Here's the oil," Paul says. "Look, I'll let you test it."

Jonah plunges the dipstick fearlessly in the open hole, and then watches as Paul declares it clean.

Paul deposits Jonah in the plane, in the copilot's seat. He puts Jonah's hands on the yoke. "This is the yoke. It steers the plane," he says.

"This is the yoke. It steers the plane," repeats Jonah, his echo planting the information in his mind.

"This is the throttle. It helps put fuel in the engine."

"Put fuel in the engine."

Their hands on the matching controls look remarkably similar, both wide and strong for their ages. Pilot, twenty-three; copilot, three.

They go over the radios, the principle of lift. Jonah is seriously absorbed. He catches sight of the back seat and demands, "I got to sit back there." He examines the seat, handles, and view.

Forty minutes have passed. "Jonah, time to go," I tell him.

"Bye, Paul," he says, easily surrendering. His rapt attention has tired him.

I have no commonality with this man of tender age, with no kids, no wife, no inkling of my pain. But he called a perfect stranger and altered his schedule for a child he will never see again. I smile at him, thank him again, and wish him the best in life.

Before I reach the first stoplight, Jonah is asleep. I wonder if this small imprinting will stay with him, make him gravitate toward airplanes instead of vacuum cleaners. But it's not about that anymore. Paul responded to a need, without calculations and wariness. He helped me leave the woman in the store behind. I hope Paul will remember us, as we will him. A blue day, a blue-eyed boy, and a mother with a face full of gratitude.

Christina Adams

"Flying" has been excerpted from *A Real Boy: A True Story of Autism, Early Intervention and Recovery*, 2005, Berkley Books/ Penguin USA. It has been edited slightly for publication in *A Cup of Comfort for Parents of Children with Autism*.

Sara's First Friend

The gray sidewalks that border my daughter's school playground are filled with chalk drawings. Today, the kindergarten chalk artists have yet to begin their detailed daily pastel drawings. As we enter the playground area, my daughter, Samantha, her red ponytails bouncing, runs ahead to place her backpack in line outside her classroom door. Sara, her little sister, slows the quick pace of her walker as she looks down, studying the chalk-filled walkways with interest.

Finally, as Sara and I reach the end of the long sidewalk, we find our place. Leaning against the wall that parallels the playground, we watch the five-year-olds as they laugh and play, tease and cry, releasing their early morning energy before another day in class.

Sara studies her sister from afar. Sara's eyes reveal nothing. I am tired this morning, as usual, because of Sara's restlessness throughout the night. Wearing blue jeans and my favorite Gap T-shirt, I sit "criss-cross applesauce" style, clutching my commuter mug. I drink the hot coffee greedily as I mentally double-check my morning routine, worried that I have forgotten something essential for Samantha's day at school. Worried, as usual, that she has not received her due share of affection or enough attention because of Sara's demanding needs. This is my morning routine. Sitting here, staring at my very different daughters, trying to imagine Sara on this playground two years from now, and questioning what our future will be.

I have mastered the role of being Sara's advocate. I believe this is inexplicitly entwined with the responsibility of being her mother. I think back for a moment when life was simple, when I was more carefree . . . before my heart began to hurt, before that life-defining moment. I was in the shower, that day, indulging in the extravagant luxury of deep-conditioning my hair. Samantha, then three, came to pound on the glass shower door. She was demanding milk in the "I want it now, Mommy!" typical toddler way. That's when it clicked: *Something is wrong with Sara.* She was sixteen months old, and not talking, not walking, and not demanding or even requesting anything. She was much delayed.

It took a year to get physicians to pay attention. I flew across the country and sought the care of a special neurologist at the Cleveland Clinic. The primary diagnosis is mitochondrial disease; the secondary neurological diagnosis, autistic spectrum, followed later that year.

On this early morning, my daughters are separated by 20 feet of sidewalk and 10 square feet of playground sand. But I know of the other very real and vast differences that place my daughters' worlds apart. Although Sara's physical disability is visible, her neurological issues are not. Sara uses a walker to lend strength to her weakened muscles. There is, however, no crutch or physical aide to help her with her autistic features. There is no outward sign to tell others that she has a neurological impairment, a different weakness with unique challenges of its own. She experiences anxiety, awkwardness, and behavior challenges. She can be very uncooperative. These are the things that cause other mothers to look, whisper, and even comment, offering unsolicited advice.

When the first morning school bell rings, Samantha runs over to us and kisses Sara and me goodbye—a wet sloppy kiss on the mouth for me and a nose rub for Sara. Samantha has learned that Sara prefers this softer, less sensory-offensive gesture of affection. With a quick wave tossed over her shoulder, Samantha runs off to collect her backpack and enter her classroom. Sara stands quietly as she watches her sister walk away. She looks at her feet as she shuffles them repeatedly. I wonder for a moment whether this is how it will always be between them: Samantha rushing off to experience life, while Sara stays behind.

Each morning as we stand against this wall, I watch Sara watching Samantha play, and every morning I wish for the same thing. I wish that, someday, Sara will be comfortable in an environment like this. I hope that this exposure to Samantha's school world will ignite Sara's interest, light a social spark.

Sara is blessed to have many "friends" in her life, people outside our home that truly care about her, want the best for her, and have great confidence in her abilities. There is Robin, Sara's speech therapist, Atalie, her physical therapist, and Michelle, her occupational therapist. Not only do these friends teach her physical skills to strengthen her muscles, they also teach her how to play with toys, initiate social interaction, follow routines, and respond socially in simple situations. Abilities her sister developed naturally, these are skills Sara will have to learn.

Today, Sara points to the children rushing by us and says "me." Surprised and excited, I bend down and look into her face. Eye to eye, I question the meaning of this spontaneous use of language. I am on my knees, waiting patiently for Sara to show me what she meant. I feel a tap on my back, and I turn and stand up to greet our neighbor, Tracy, and her three-year-old little girl, Katie.

We all drift toward the parking lot. Katie is running in circles and humming loudly. For a few minutes, I am lost in simple conversation with Tracy.

We talk of our husbands' long work hours, recipes for gourmet dinners, and dirty laundry, and I feel as though I am miles away from the complex therapy schedules, vitamin supplements, medical bills, and emotional worry that fill my world. I am a typical mom, just beginning my day, standing in the school parking lot, visiting with a neighbor, carefree.

Relaxed and preparing to say goodbye, I look down at Sara. She's been walking beside us in her walker, quietly regarding Tracy and Katie. Suddenly, she is leaning against her walker for balance, and Katie is reaching for Sara's hand, and for a moment Sara lets her hold it. Then, amazingly, she leans toward Katie and rubs her nose to the tip of hers. An Eskimo kiss; she imitates the kiss goodbye her sister gave her a few minutes ago.

The sun shines brightly, and I am shielding my eyes from the glare. My fingers form a half fortress wall, protecting the tears that are pooling in my eyes. I feel warmth in my chest, and I recognize this unfamiliar feeling as unexpected joy. It leaves me with a sense of contentment, yet I feel strangely energized.

In a gesture of celebration and hope, I put my arm around Tracy's shoulders and pull her into a hug. I lean down and brush Sara's cheek lightly with my lips. Her rosebud lips offer me a subtle, shy smile. And I know that she knows. Sara has found her first friend.

Suzanne M. Perryman

What Comes Next?

"I want my school!" howled my four-year-old son, Jack, in full-blown tantrum mode. He kicked the back of my seat and punched the air. "No more car ride! I want my school!"

"We have to drop off your sister first, honey," I said, envious of my ten-year-old daughter, Hailey, who sat beside me with her hands over her ears. As my daughter hurried out of the car, she shouted over her brother's wails, "We need to buy ear plugs, Mom." I winced in agreement.

My son, who was diagnosed with Asperger's two years earlier, believes trips in the car should serve a single purpose—to get him from point A to point B as quickly as possible. When we try to combine more than one stop into the same trip, he expresses his displeasure at a volume that rattles the car windows.

Five minutes of screaming later, I pulled into a parking slot at Jack's preschool with a sigh of relief and released my son from his car seat. He wiped his eyes on his sleeve, grabbed my hand, and took off for the front door at a dead run, as though he'd escaped from the gullet of a ravenous monster. With my ears still ringing, I followed him into the building, wishing I could take the trauma out of traveling for my little boy.

Jack's tense expression relaxed when he entered the peaceful, tidy classroom. He hung his backpack on a hook labeled with his name, checked his cubby, and gave his teacher a hug. As his teacher and I chatted, Jack walked over to the class activity calendar. Pointing to a picture of toys, he asked the teacher, "Now playtime?"

"That's right, Jack," she said, and he grinned and ran to the toy chest. "He loves knowing what's next," his teacher said with a chuckle.

"I know how he feels," I said, "I'd be lost without my planner." *Wait*, I thought. *Is it possible that Jack's problem is something as simple as wanting to know what comes next?*

I excused myself and left, my thoughts churning. *Maybe Jack hated our trips in the car because they brought unwelcome surprises. Perhaps he craved the stability and organization of a schedule. He couldn't read, so a standard planner wouldn't help, but he has always been highly visual and social stories work well for him. What about a traveling picture book?*

Inspired, I spent the next three hours glued to the viewfinder of my digital camera. I collected images of the gas station, the schools, the church, the grocery stores, and other common destinations. I bought a child-size photo album, printed out the pictures, stuffed them in a manila envelope, and taped the envelope to the back of the album. I put a picture of Jack's preschool on the first page, followed by a picture of our car, his car seat, his favorite fast food restaurant, and last of all, a picture of our home. The picture planner was ready to go.

I picked up Jack from preschool and showed him his new planner. "This is a picture of your school; we're here now. Next," I said as I turned to each of the corresponding pages, "we're going to get in the car, then we're going to get French fries, and then we're going to go home."

Bemused, my son flipped the album pages. I wasn't sure whether he understood, but when I showed him the picture of his car seat and asked him what came next, he said, "I get in car seat." He climbed in without a fuss.

As I pulled out of the preschool driveway, I asked him what came next, and he said, "We get French fries?"

"That's right!" I told him, beaming. We picked up our snack and drove home, all without a murmur of discontent from the back seat.

My son still occasionally puts up minor resistance to car trips, which takes the form of surreptitious picture removal and replacement ("No, Mommy, see? Not the bank, next get ice cream!"), but overall the system has worked like a quiet, peaceful dream. For the effort of spending a few minutes setting up his book every morning, I have been rewarded with a cheerful, confident child.

A few months after we started using the book, I was asked to attend an important conference out of town. I wasn't sure how to explain my days-long absence to my son. I mentioned my dilemma to a friend, and she said, "Couldn't you use another version of his picture planner?"

I knew my son's first question the night I left would be, "Where's Mommy?" so that's what I named the new picture book. With my husband's help, I gathered pictures of myself driving away, pictures of the hotel where the conference would be held, pictures of the sun and pictures of the moon and stars for each day and night I'd be gone, and a picture of myself returning home, and put them all in an album.

The day I was to leave, I handed my son the new book and went over it with him. "Mommy has to take a car ride to a special class; she'll be gone a night and a day and a night and a day, and then Mommy will be home again." He looked through the pages and "read" it back to me. I hugged him, handed him off to his father, and left.

When I arrived at my destination, I called home and asked my husband how Jack was doing. "Is he all right? Does he miss me?"

"He's asked where you are, and each time the girls and I read him his "Where's Mommy?" book, and he settles down. He hasn't cried once."

Before hanging up, my husband put Jack on the phone. "Hello, Mommy," he chirped. "You're gone at the class, and gone this night and this day and this night and this day, and then you'll come home to me! See?"

"Yes," I told him, so proud tears pricked my eyes, "I do see."

Growing up is hard work, and the world can be a confusing place, especially for someone with a processing disorder. While I can't change the world for my son, I can give him the tools he needs to puzzle things out for himself. And that gives me hope.

Heather Jensen

A Is for Ability

My stepson, Alp, and I sit at the conference table in the office of the Center for Family Wellness. We are about to have an intake interview to find out what services they might provide for him and the rest of our family.

Alp has autism, and his speech is very delayed. He is, however, verbal, so I want him to participate in the interview as much as possible.

The friendly-faced lady comes in to greet us, shuffling her pile of paperwork in order to shake our hands.

"Welcome!" she says cheerily. "My name is Kathy, and I'm a counselor here. I'll be asking you some questions today."

I stand for the handshake and tell her my name. Alp does not rise, so Kathy leans over to offer the greeting.

Alp knows what to do: He extends his hand for her to shake his floppy arm.

"What's your name?" She encourages his participation.

"My name is Alp," he answers perfectly, albeit with his monotone, almost parrot-like intonation.

I smile with pride at his good answer.

Kathy explains that she will be asking a lot of questions and taking notes. Some of the questions will be for Alp. She looks to Alp for agreement, but he is already focused on something of more interest to him—a strip of paper on the floor.

"What's that string machine?" He asks me, oblivious not only to Kathy's question but also to her very existence.

The "machine" part of the question is his latest speech oddity. These come and go with approximately three-week intervals. Recently, he started to arbitrarily add the word machine after just about every noun: dog machine, pencil machine, pasta machine, you name it. I'm guessing this one has something to do with his recent favorite toy, the gumball machine.

I dive under the table to retrieve the paper strip and hand it to Alp. Then, straightening up in my chair, I try to resume some modicum of dignity and apologize to Kathy.

"I'm sorry. He really loves string-like things," I explain. "That will keep him happy for now."

Kathy seems unfazed and begins to ask Alp some questions. All the while, Alp holds either end of the "string machine" in his hands and lets the string grow slack and then quickly tightens it to make it snap, over and over again, while staring at its middle. He is stimming (self-stimulating behavior).

"How old are you, Alp?" Kathy sits poised with her pen, ready to fill in her questionnaire blanks.

"I'm nine years old," Alp recites, without taking his eyes off of the moving paper strip.

I interrupt. "Alp, you are not nine," as if that was just some funny joke. At this size, he would be a monster of a nine-year-old!

Kathy scratches out the wrong answer.

"I'm eight years old!"

"Alp!" I protest, as if to tell him to stop joking around. In reality, I'm trying to jolt him into participation.

"I'm seven, I'm six, I'm five . . ."

Kathy stops writing. We both grow silent and turn our eyes to Alp. The quiet brings him back to us, and he understands that we will not leave him alone with this string until we get a reasonable reply.

"I'm eleven years old."

"Very good," Kathy starts to write on her pad again. "When is your birthday, Alp?"

This answer shoots out like a cannonball. "June twenty-nine, nineteen-ninety-four."

Kathy looks impressed. Of course, I know that if she were to ask, "When is your dog going to fly to the moon?" his answer would be the same. Most *when* questions merit the birth date response.

"Do you have any brothers and sisters?" she asks next.

Now, Alp is ripping the paper strip into tiny pieces and lining them up on the table. "Yes"

"What are their names?"

"Mrs. Platt."

Of course, none of my daughters has that name. *Mrs. Platt* is the standard reply to any question involving the words *name* or *who*.

"Alp," I tried to help, "Mrs. Platt was your teacher last year. Kathy wants to know your sisters' names."

"No! What are their names?" He says sternly, which also means, I'm not taking any further questions. Next, he raises his voice a bit to demand, "I want to go home."

I try to calmly explain that we will go home soon, but we have to answer a few more questions before that will be possible. If he is a good boy, I offer, we will stop at Burger King on the way home. This is a valuable reward, and it may buy us a few more good minutes.

"Yes, go to Burger King," he responds to accept the offer.

Kathy lets him off the hook then, realizing he is becoming agitated. I explain that verbal communication does not come easily for him. He avoids it whenever there is any other option. As for answering questions, he seems to have stored up a handful of standard responses that he spits out in order to avoid what can be a difficult process for him. I imagine it's much like it would be were someone to ask me to spontaneously crank out complex mathematical equations.

Sadly, the standard answers Alp shoots out are often wrong. For example, in the car on the way to the interview, we passed a field of cows, and I asked him to identify the animal he was looking at out the window. Of course, he knows cows, has known them since he was a toddler, but it didn't surprise me when he answered with his latest standard animal-question response: "Penguin."

Unfortunately, how one speaks is often equated with one's intelligence. With Alp, as with many kids who have autism or similar pervasive development disorders, verbal ability is typically unrelated to intelligence.

Near the conclusion of our intake interview, however, Alp uses language to show off an ability Kathy and I could never dream of mastering. As I answer one of the last questions, Alp interrupts to ask, "Who's calling on the phone?"

I know what this means, so I grab my purse from the back of the chair, take out my cell phone, and set it on the table. About thirty seconds later, it rings. Alp's ability to feel or hear the signal before a phone actually rings is something we've grown accustomed to at our house. Kathy, however, has never seen such a thing before.

Now it is Kathy, not Alp, who is at a loss for words!

Lauren Finaldi Gürus

 Sophie's Song

A five-year-old red-haired boy with a minia-
ture viola who has just finished playing his
piece bows to the parents and children who
fill the stadium-style seating in the university classroom. The emcee announces that the next Suzuki
string program performer is Sophie Wigney, who will
be playing "Twinkle, Twinkle, Little Star."

Sophie, who is almost eight years old, gets up
from the front row where she has been sitting with
the other children who are recital performers this
Saturday morning and takes her place at the front of
the room. Her dark hair is pulled back at the temples
but hangs long past her shoulders and down her back,
draping her loose, burgundy patterned dress.

As she fidgets her way into a proper violin-playing
stance, her parents wait nervously for her performance:
Richard's sweaty hands are tightly gripping Patricia's.
She is in tears almost before Sophie begins.

There are five variations of "Twinkle" in *Suzuki Violin Book One*. Children who start this book when Sophie did, at age four, typically finish it within six months. It has taken Sophie three years; Sophie has autism.

Sophie developed typically for the first two years of her life. Then suddenly at age two, soon after a severe reaction to her MMR vaccination sent her into an extended period of fevers and mouth blisters, she stopped babbling and interacting. The diagnosis of "high-functioning autism" was given a year later.

Patricia was devastated by the diagnosis, but she was determined to give Sophie every experience she could, including filling her daughter's life with music. When Sophie was four, Richard found a local music therapist for her, and after only a few lessons, Sophie not only was saying her own name for the first time but was also singing the spelling as well. This gave Patricia the determination to keep her involved in various forms of music, and Patricia soon approached the Suzuki string program her older daughters had attended.

For Sophie, the process has been slow but incremental. In the second year of violin lessons, she was still learning how to stand and hold the bow. Like many children with autism, she has difficulty with coordination. Making her body parts all move independently and in sync takes intense concentration. Leaning her head in an unnatural position and into the chin rest of the violin and holding her left arm outward and her right arm up are challenging tasks in themselves, over and beyond learning to play the instrument.

The most difficult part for Debby, Sophie's violin teacher, has been helping Sophie to learn without correcting her mistakes. Sophie's perfectionism manifests itself in extreme form due to the autism. Nothing can be "difficult." Sophie does not need "help"—although, occasionally she will accept "assistance." If other verbiage is used, Sophie spirals into trauma, "Why do you ask if I need help? I don't need help! I'm fine!" The anxiety she experiences tightens her vocal cords; the pitch of her voice becomes a high, tense singing tone like that made by an overstrung bow. Once she is upset in this way, she often gets stuck, seemingly unable to let go of the irritation. "Did you hear me?" she'll continue, "Why did you ask if I need help? I don't need help. Understand?"

So instead of correcting mistakes, Debby learned to use Sophie's penchant for imaginary play to teach her. For example, when Sophie was fixated on *Thomas the Tank*, Debby explained that Sophie's wrist was part of a train track that ran down her arm. The wrist needed to be straight in order for Thomas to stay on the track.

Debby is a petite woman with wiry curly dark hair laced with silver, and she walks with a limp due to multiple sclerosis. At one point, she felt overwhelmed by her teaching schedule and decided to drop all of her students but one: Sophie. With a degree in school psychology, Debby wanted to work with a child with special needs, and she felt she could truly have an impact on Sophie's life. Since the violin lessons took place at Sophie's house, she could also help Sophie work on another skill that is difficult because of her autism: transitioning from one activity to the next. The two ease into each lesson by first reading a book or playing a game.

One day Sophie invited Debby to jump on the trampoline with her before the lesson. Debby explained that it would be very hard for her to do.

"Why would it be hard for you?" asked Sophie.

The two discussed Debby's limp; Debby showed Sophie her brace and even let Sophie wear it during the lesson. Sophie seemed to understand. The difficulty of playing the violin for her was like jumping on the trampoline for Debby.

Over a few years, Sophie gradually learned "Twinkle, Twinkle, Little Star." At first, Debby made individual three-by-five-inch cards showing one note each, with a photograph of the correct fingering for that note. Sophie learned the song by playing a single note at a time, sometimes only one note during a whole lesson. The cards eventually gave way to a poster with the notes written in lines and with each of the six lines of the song denoted by a sticker: Winnie the Pooh, a rabbit, a star, a grasshopper, a violin, and finally Tigger.

During the last year or so, Patricia had worked with Sophie with the goal of getting through a single line.

"Ready? Let's play the grasshoppa!" she would say in a silly voice to make Sophie giggle.

Last month, Sophie played each line in sequence for the first time and finally seemed to realize it was a song. Patricia and Debby decided Sophie was ready for her first recital. They thought she could handle playing a single line and had Sophie practice a few times: bow to the audience, play the Pooh line, bow again. But Sophie had other ideas. She insisted she was going to play the whole song.

Now, Sophie stands poised, ready to play in her first recital. Debby, in the front row, unrolls the music poster. But Sophie doesn't want the musical text; she doesn't want help.

"Don't roll that out! Just roll it up like it was," she insists as the packed classroom of parents and children watch in silence.

Debby hastily rerolls the poster in the hope that Sophie won't fixate on the error. But Sophie is focused on her violin. She begins.

"Twink-le, twink-le, lit-tle star," sings the violin.

Sophie pauses.

"Well done, Sophie!" says the emcee and begins to clap, at which the audience responds with polite applause.

"Not yet!" hollers Sophie over the din, exasperated.

The clapping wanes, and Patricia half-stands from her third row seat and loudly whispers to the emcee, "She wants to play the whole thing." Meanwhile, she's thinking to herself, *Sophie, please don't throw the violin.*

Sophie returns to playing, a bit distracted by the interruption. The first notes are slightly sharp:

"How I won-der what you are . . ." The melody becomes more hesitant, staggered with pauses, and some notes slide prematurely into the next:

"Up a-bove the world so high . . ."

Then the lines of music become confused:

"Twink-le, twink-le, above the world, like a . . ."

Sophie pauses again, pulls her left hand away from the neck of the violin, and touches her thumb to each of her four fingers, trying to remember which line comes next.

"Just repeat the Pooh line," whispers Debby.

Sophie responds loudly in a high, tight, crying voice, emphatic with stress: "It's not the Pooh line. I'm done with Pooh Bear! Which one of the other ones?"

Pooh is the first "Twinkle" verse, and the violin is the second verse. The notes of each line are exact duplicates, but Patricia knows Sophie hasn't made that connection; she knows Sophie needs to be told to play the violin line.

Patricia notices the man in the seat in front of her as he adjusts his position and sighs impatiently. She can only imagine what he is thinking: *What a spoiled brat.* Little does he know that, while Sophie looks like a typical eight-year-old girl, this whole experience—the noise, the people, let alone the performance itself—is a stress load that can easily overwhelm a child with autism, leading to either complete withdrawal or full-blown tantrum. Little does he realize that though Sophie is struggling, she is dealing with the stress. She is coping.

Meanwhile, Debby unrolls Sophie's music poster, and Sophie, undaunted, starts the second "Twinkle" verse marked by the violin sticker, playing through it perfectly:

"Twink-le, twink-le, lit-tle star . . ."

"Almost done!" Sophie calls sweetly to the crowd.

"How I won-der what you are."

The room fills with applause, and Sophie beams. She forgets to bow or even to leave the stage, and the audience responds by continuing to clap. She is filled with awe. "Wow," Sophie says aloud, smiling as she takes it all in. "Wow."

Afterward, Debby and Patricia hug tightly and cry, each one thinking how much this moment means to the other.

Sophie comes up beside them. "Now maybe you can jump on the trampoline," she says to Debby.

"Now that you've had your first recital, maybe I can," muses Debbie.

"You don't have to be scared," Sophie says gently. "I'll be right beside you the whole time."

Tabitha Thompson

A Vehicle of Change

"We'll be leaving in ten minutes," I warn my son. His ritual begins.

"Two-thousand-two Ford Escort, automatic transmission, four doors, low mileage, air conditioning, CD player, immaculate condition. 2001 Honda Passport, automatic transmission, four-wheel drive, leather seats, sunroof, every possible option. 1998 Toyota Camry XLE . . ."

For most people, the ability of a six-year-old to recite a detailed list of cars and features from memory is impressive. For me, this routine grates on my nerves like brakes that squeal. J. P.'s repetitive custom reminds me of my failure as a mother. For, even though experts do not know the direct cause of Asperger's syndrome, my gut tells me that my DNA has passed this on to my son. Much of the obsessive, compulsive, and anti-social behavior I witness daily in J. P. displayed itself in my father while I was growing up. I feel guilty for having reproduced this legacy. I feel anger at the cyclical nature of the Universe.

As my son continues orating, he over-articulates each word and stresses every other syllable with great intensity. J. P. paces his room with a jerky step-hop. He twists the fingers of each hand into contorted claws, pressing his fingers so tightly that his knuckles glow bright white. This is what my son does when he is excited. This is what he does when he's sad. This is what he does when he's happy, anxious, nervous, or fearful. And this is what I'm witnessing for the third time today.

"Five more minutes," I say, as I help my younger son, Luc, put on his sneakers. At three years old, Luc displays the "normal" qualities of a typical boy. He enjoys toy cars but likes many other playthings as well. He transitions easily from one activity to another, lives in the present, and is demonstratively affectionate. J. P., however, only plays with cars and has no interest in trying a toy or game that he cannot turn into a car-related object. He consistently lives in the future and needlessly worries himself over what will come next, whether it might be hours or days away. If I wait until the last minute to tell J. P. about an upcoming event in the hopes of sparing him undo anxiety, he rages into a tantrum. My warped sense of logic says that my firstborn, J. P., soaked up all my family's angst genes in utero, leaving Luc to inherit the more laid-back genes of my husband's family.

J. P. comes out of his room carrying three Auto Mart magazines, the ones that are handed out free at the grocery store.

"No car magazines," I say as gently as possible. "We're going to help Madeleine celebrate her birthday, not talk about cars."

"Can I bring my *Car & Driver* magazine?"

"Not this time."

"But Mommy, I want to read Madeleine the article about the all new 2005 Chevrolet Equinox. . . . "

I would love to allow my son to show off one of the few advantages of his Asperger's. (He taught himself to read by age three and now reads at a fourth-grade level.) But if he brings the magazine, he definitely won't use this party as a place to practice the social skills he has been learning. Besides, I am desperate for a car-free afternoon. "No car magazines of any kind."

"Can we go to the party in the Monte Carlo?"

"No."

"Why not?"

"Because that's Daddy's car, and he needs it to go to work."

"So we're taking the Saturn SL1?"

"Obviously," I retort.

"Can we drive by Inskip Auto Mall so I can see my BMWs?"

"No!" I don't mean to shout. I know that raising my voice at my sensitive son will cause him to panic and withdraw, but after a morning of walking around a local car dealership (his favorite special treat), playing Matchbox car dealership, and watching some NASCAR racing on TV, my "good Mommy" fuel tank is on empty.

I muster all the patience I can. "I'm sorry," I say calmly, "Mommy shouldn't yell. That was a bad choice. I know you're nervous about going to Madeleine's house. If you put on your sneakers and get in the car, I'll let you read the Saturn owner's manual to me while I drive."

My peace treaty diffuses the time bomb of anxiety ticking in J. P., and on the way to the party, I learn about my car's cruise control and air conditioning features.

Upon arriving at the party, J. P. names every car lined in front of the birthday girl's house and peers into each one to check out its features. When Madeleine greets him at the door, he recites a new litany of car names and features.

"Remember, honey," I whisper with firmness, "not everyone likes to talk about cars all the time."

Madeleine, who knows J. P. so well, hands him her few Hot Wheels cars, then takes Luc to join party games with the other children. J. P. remains in the corner of an empty room, contentedly playing alone. Yet, every once in a while, he stands in the doorway, watching the other kids at play, mumbling car facts, and gently rocking back and forth. Part of him wants to interact with the group. He wants to participate. But despite the hours of social skills work he's done with me and with his therapist, he's not able to join the noisy group. After a full hour, J. P. is ready to interact with another person. He chooses the birthday girl's aunt and uses his best pickup line: "What kind of car do you drive?"

J. P. feels comfortable with adults. Adults are predictable, quiet, and calm. When an adult realizes he speaks at a grown-up level, the person lavishes attention on him, praising his gentle spirit and marveling at his intelligence. The positive feedback he receives sends him on a high that boosts his ego and grants him confidence. Unfortunately, it also perpetuates his reluctance to form friendships with children his own age, who do not care about his advanced reading and speaking skills or his passion for cars.

"Your son asked me for my phone number," Madeleine's aunt tells me later. "Apparently he wants to be able to call me up to talk about cars sometime."

Suddenly, I fear for my son's future prom date, whom I'm guessing will be Madeleine, one of the few kids who seems to understand him. I picture her sitting next to him in the Chevy Monte Carlo (the one he hopes to inherit from his daddy someday) parked at the top of make-out hill. He leans over. She thinks he's about to kiss her. Instead, he takes the owner's manual out of the glove compartment and shows her pictures of the car's anti-lock braking system.

"He's amazing," Madeleine's aunt continues, "so well-mannered and incredibly smart. You've done a great job raising him."

Snippets of my creative parenting flash before my eyes. I made him a car puppet to show him how to talk with other people. I created an intricate pattern of car-related stickers on a chalkboard to teach him to write capital letters. I pointed out facial expressions and nonverbal communications of race car drivers to coach him about empathy. I have given him countless *Auto Mart* magazines as rewards for good behavior and have taken numerous ones away as consequences for bad behavior.

Most important, I have worked hard on myself. I have learned to keep patient way beyond my boiling point, to find creative alternatives to problems, and to speak up in the face of authority. I have given up on the notion of being perfect or having perfect children. I am still working on my control issues. The difficulties I've faced with J. P. help me appreciate the relative ease of raising Luc, and I continually strive to prevent J. P.'s issues from robbing all my time and attention. I am learning the power of unconditional love.

To navigate the long and winding road of Asperger's syndrome means we work with an incomplete map and poorly marked street signs. Potholes dot our highway, changing lanes takes extra care, and gridlock all too often slows us down. But we have strapped ourselves into a safe vehicle called Faith and believe that our travels will carry us in the right direction. In the meantime, we will take time to enjoy the views of a journey that will change us all for the better.

Judy L. Adourian

The Offering

My father is dying. The phone rings, and I steel myself for the inevitable.

My brother's voice is strained as we exchange small talk, and then he hesitates.

"I'm sorry," he begins. "I'm afraid I have sad news for you."

"Is it Pop?" Tension courses through me, exploding at my temples.

"No. No." He clears his throat. "It isn't Pop." Another pause. "Our mama died today."

"M-Mom?" I stutter. "It can't—I mean—there must—"

"I'm sorry," my brother repeats.

Stunned into silence, I fall onto the bed as the phone slides from my fingers. My ears refuse to listen, my mind to comprehend. It cannot be. It cannot be. And yet it is.

Burrowing into a nest of pillows and down, I cry, silently at first and then in gulping sobs. A room away, Ryan is napping, curled in upon himself, a man-child in a world apart. Obscured for more than two decades by the dark curtain of autism, he gives no indication of waking to the anguish reverberating around him. Afternoon sunlight spills across his sleeping face and pools on the carpet around him. By the time he wakes, the house is awash in the business of grieving.

"Hey, Ryan." His sister's warm greeting brings Ryan's gaze into focus momentarily. She runs her hand across his forehead, pushing back his hair. "Let's go fix something to eat."

Thunk! Ryan pops the recliner upright and bolts for the kitchen. He throws open the freezer and grabs a box of ice cream bars.

Skilled by time and devotion, Emma redirects him. "After dinner," she bargains. "We'll have ice cream after dinner."

"After," he repeats, his hands still locked around the box. "After dinner," he reassures himself, loosening his grip.

As she slips the box into the freezer, Emma looks away. "I think we'll have . . . Let's see what's in the cupboard." By the time she turns around, Ryan is helping himself to a can of leftover icing. Emma manages a smile.

"Ah-ha-ha," she teases, "Ya tricked me, didn't ya? Yeah, well, okay, let's put that away for another time."

He pauses, giving her a measured glance. "Another time," he echoes.

"How about a salad, Ryan?" Emma asks, forgetting this is Ryan's produce phase.

Within seconds, tunnel vision takes over. Ryan flies through the produce bin, rummaging and tossing. Giant tomatoes and ruffled leaf lettuce land in the garbage. Ryan's compulsion to gather things and stuff them in containers is as familiar as the sun in the afternoon sky. But his compulsions morph; they constantly evolve from one form to another. Just when things seem to be settling down, you get ambushed. A month ago it was the laundry. Blankets, sheets, and clean shirts hanging in the closet were spirited away, showing up in kitchen cupboards, underneath the bathroom sink, packed away in luggage. Gather and contain. And now it's produce.

Emma takes a breath. Directly interfering in Ryan's gathering routine invariably sends him into shrieks of rebellion and distress. "Okay, Ryan," Emma keeps an even voice. "Let's take a break," she leads him to the rocking chair. "And then we'll fix dinner."

By evening, the overwhelming obligations of a funeral bear down. The house is filled with a cacophony of ringing phones, muffled crying, and exhausted voices.

"I just vacuum," the familiar hum of Ryan's voice rises and falls as he wanders the house, seemingly oblivious to the sea of activity and grief around him. Emma keeps his routine going.

At bedtime, I brush my hand along his cheek. "Ryan, Grandma died," I say.

"Grandma died," he echoes. Then, "I just vacuum tomorrow."

At the cemetery Ryan wanders to the edge of the trees, treasuring up sticks and pinecones and then laying them on the ground in piles to be trundled off to barrels later on. With aching familiarity, the ritual begins. Gather, contain. All the efforts of medicine and man have failed to bring this life-stopping compulsion into full submission. While prayers are said and wreaths are laid, piles of sticks and pinecones multiply.

Lingering in the lilac-ringed cemetery, we stand together for a family photo. The final image tells our story. We lean together, pressed around our son and brother as he struggles to cope within the confines of his own compulsions. His body is tense, poised to spring. His eyes are locked on the distant trees, zeroed in on twigs and pine needles scattered on the ground.

There is stillness as we drive away. And then it starts again. Tufts of lint. He gathers them into his hand. The long drive home is solemn. Exhausted by the week's ordeal, I long to rest, but sense there is more to come. Within two days my brother calls again.

"It's Pop," he says. "He's in a coma."

Ryan, expressionless, rocks beside his papa's bed. Later, Emma talks to him, tells him Grandpa is dying. She speaks to him at length, choosing words that do not compromise the possibility that Ryan understands. Two days later, Pop is gone. "Ryan, Grandpa died," we tell him gently. He turns away, looking for a lost CD.

My father was a complicated man. No one knew him; no one understood him. Just when you thought you were having a conversation, he'd get up and leave. And so it was an odd connection that formed between the two of them, Ryan and my father. Ryan's unexpected inroads took my father by surprise, made him smile.

One winter day my father brooded silently, and for a brief moment, Ryan's words connected. "Papa, you just need to get your pajamas on and go to bed," he blurted, and then his words were gone. Caught off guard, my father hadn't time to quell his wonder before his voice careened in startled laughter.

One September morning before my father died, I lost myself beneath the cover of a book, tuning out the white noise of Ryan's repetitious chatter. "Happy birthday, Ryan," he greeted himself a hundred times that morning. "Happy birthday," he persisted, though his birthday was half a year away. It was nearly afternoon when his voice made its way into my consciousness again. "Happy birthday," Ryan echoed softly to himself as he stood rocking at the window, gazing into space. "Happy—" Click. The wires in my mental calendar connected. September third. My father's eighty-second birthday.

That was then, of course. A million years ago. Today the rain stops somewhere between the chapel and the cemetery. The clouds thin out, like cotton candy pulled apart. A half-sun washes over us. I steady Ryan as the sounds of military rites play out. Rifle shots split the air. Ryan is restless, but unflinching. Then he turns. Again, he wanders to the edge of the trees and begins sifting through the fallen sticks and pinecones.

At the gravesite, there is milling about, hugging, conversing, and a cappella singing. I stand in a huddle with my sister's family. Ryan is forgotten, a silent shadow on the fringes of this solemn day. Gradually, my father's progeny form into a softly curving line, each stepping forward in their turn to say a last farewell. Roses and carnations slip from gnarled hands and tiny fingers onto the coffin's gleaming wood. As the last offering is laid, I sense

Ryan at my side, feel the knitted softness of a sweater brush my arm. Instinctively, I turn.

Against all expectations, Ryan is here, where he belongs. He stands frozen, his eyes fixed. Awkwardly he walks toward his papa's grave. Reaching out gently, his man's hand shaking, he lays his treasure down. Atop the burnished poplar rests a grandson's solemn offering: a single, perfect pinecone. Ryan pauses, his eyes shining with rare untarnished clarity. Then he fades and pulls away. His awkward gait carries him toward the trees as shadows roll beneath the clouds, closing up the sunlight, hiding up the heavens once again.

Rebekah Schow

Ryan and Emma are pseudonyms chosen by the author, who has also used a pseudonym, in order to preserve her children's anonymity.

Outside Inside the Box

I smile as I tuck my son into his cozy car bed, hoping that with some good music and a little melatonin he will motor himself to sleep. I remember when bedtime was very different, when our son became different. Upon his diagnosis at age three, we arrived in a new town shocked and shattered but with the hope that an established autism program would "fix" our little boy. We were strangers to our city, our environment, and most crucially, our son. What a difference a label makes. The child I had cuddled and tickled and warbled to just a few weeks before now seemed foreign to me. I recall just staring at him as he sat in his high chair, a containment device, bewildered at the task ahead. I no longer knew what to feed him (after learning he was allergic to virtually everything), what to say to him (he'd lost his expressive and receptive speech), or how to heal him. I couldn't even tell when he was suffering, because he'd stopped responding to physical pain. So there we were in our new kitchen, both trapped in his developing condition.

As unprepared as we were to accept our altered future, we were even less prepared to meet daily, elemental challenges. Autism has an uncanny way of making the simple complicated; our challenges, like mushrooms, sprang up and flourished in the most unexpected ways. For example, my little boy was down to eating rice and beans in the beginning, because I literally didn't know what else to feed him. He couldn't have wheat, grain, or dairy products. No soy, corn, or apple products (trust me, everything has either corn syrup or apple in it). So I was thrust into the world of rice and legumes. Fortunately, the managers of the local health food stores taught me everything I ever wanted to know about rice products but was afraid to ask. They also guided me through the heady world of alternative cooking.

In addition to the cuisine question, another confounding challenge we faced, like so many autistic families, was how to keep our son in bed at night. This one required my husband's dogged persistence. Josh was happily arising at three or four in the morning, trotting downstairs, and blasting music out of my husband's complex stereo system. (Smart kid; I still can't work the stereo system.) He was also sneaking into the kitchen and stealing away with everything we feared would kill him—yogurt, muffins, and apple juice. After quickly decorating the kitchen doors and all the doors in the house with hooks 'n eyes, we were still trumped by the sleep disturbances. How could we keep Joshie asleep and in bed? That was the question we faced every night. Reluctantly, we realized that bed was not the operational word. Neither was crib. Much to my dismay, my husband and I resorted to an unconventional solution.

It took Jeff about three days to construct "The Box." I sobbed when he completed it, appalled at the mere idea of it and horrified once again by the confines of autism. The tragedy was that I was experiencing déjà vu. When we'd narrowed our relocation choices to two cities, Pittsburgh or Greensboro, a gracious local Pittsburgh family agreed to let us observe their affected daughter and her program. We were impressed and dazed by what we couldn't quite comprehend so early in the game. But what hit me and sent me politely fleeing from the house was the sight of the young girl's bedroom. I stared at the large, empty box in her fluffy little chamber and whispered to my husband, "What is that? Is it a toy box?" Our hosts, sensing the confusion, explained it was where their little girl slept at night—by choice. She had sensory issues, and the box was her sleep aid. She was comfortable in it and comforted by it. My ignorance of autism created a radically opposite interpretation of what I saw. I barely made it to the rental car before I burst into tears. *What the hell was that? This little cherub was living like a caged animal. It's inhumane. What the hell is this autism anyway?* I shrieked all the way to the airport.

How ironic that a mere three months later we resorted to repeating what I thought was an ugly story. Our box was enormous. So enormous you had to use a small ladder to climb in and out of it. Jeff was incredibly proud of himself. I believe it was the first time he had ever grabbed a hammer in his life. It was much weightier than the surgical tools he was used to.

"He'll never get out of this," Jeff told me, beaming.

I wanted to hit him. And naturally, being me, I quickly tried to disguise the reality of the box with fancy blankets, comforters, and Josh's favorite toys. I even placed a fan over it for perfect ventilation. How silly we must have looked trying to staple gun a huge cotton blanket to the interior walls to protect Josh from splinters. I'm sure all he would've had to do was pick at one or two of the staples to really hurt himself. Thankfully, he didn't. And, ultimately, I believe he forgave us for our desperate, hasty actions. He even forgave us for the box.

Not without a fight, though. Despite being the tender age of three and severely autistic, my son managed to outfox my brilliant husband at every turn. The first time we planted Josh in his monstrosity for a nap, Jeff was giddy with accomplishment. I was sick with anxiety and guilt. We tiptoed downstairs, made a run for our room, and then released a collective sigh of relief. Jeff picked up his paper, and I picked my lips with anxiety. Moments later, we were understandably shocked to hear little footsteps racing down the stairs. We knew it couldn't be Jordan, Josh's typical twin sister, because she was in the playroom at the time.

"It can't be!" my husband exclaimed. "How the hell did he do that?"

Beats me. Now we had a certifiable challenge on our hands. Something no male can resist. We quickly collected Josh, who was enjoying the consternation immensely, and plopped him back in his box—"Josh in the Box"—and then we hid outside his room in the hallway.

"Shhh," Jeff said. "Let's see what he does."

We quietly peered around the corner. I'll tell you what he did. He got out. This child managed to stretch his legs out to the sides of the walls and side-step his way out backward. It was impressive to watch.

"Ah-ha!" Jeff said. "Now I'm on to you, you little . . ." The gleam in my husband's eye was matched only by the gleam in Josh's.

About two minutes later, my husband was on his fiftieth sortie to Home Depot. Josh and I played in his room together, ignoring the much-needed nap.

Triumphantly, Jeff soon returned with wooden planks in hand. "Now let's see if you can escape this!"

Josh watched with fascination as his father made another attempt at perfecting his impending incarceration. Jeff happily hook-'n-eyed three large planks across the top of the box. Ostensibly, Josh would be able to exit his fate only if we unhooked one of the planks. We plopped him in yet again and then scurried to the hallway.

"Watch this," Jeff said. "He'll never get out."

Well, I'll tell you what he did. He got out. By this time, I was so entertained by my son's genius that I was distracted from my angst.

"Hey, Einstein," I said to my husband, "he did it again."

This time Josh managed to reach up and push the slats just far enough apart to pull up and fit his head and skinny body through the space. Jeff was amazed but undaunted. Josh and I sat down together for the third time that day to amuse ourselves while Jeff scooted off to Home Depot. Eventually, he returned with what appeared to be fish netting.

"I don't even want to know what you're going to do with that," I said.

"Just watch and learn," Jeff said.

He proceeded to affix the netting over the planks that extended across the top of the box. We plopped Houdini in yet again and scurried to our spot. This time we couldn't help but laugh. When we peered around the corner, all we could see was the crown of our little boy's curly head bobbing up every now and then against the netting. He reminded us of a salmon trying to swim upstream. There was no escape. Jeff hailed it a victory. Josh didn't see it that way, telling us with loud snuffles that he wasn't happy in that box.

The good news is that, almost immediately, our son not only accepted his box, he also thrived in it. His occupational therapist explained how it provided the natural boundaries, structure, and womb-like insulation he needed while struggling with sensory issues. It was a quiet, peaceful sleep center by night and a huge toy box by day. And we didn't get arrested for it. I was always paranoid that the first stranger to behold our creation would make a mad dash for Child Protection Services and turn us in. But everyone seemed to get it. Even my mother and mother-in-law . . . once each stopped crying.

In fact, Josh's box slowly became a major attraction. I never advertised it, but the few kids who saw it thought it was awesome. And Josh's sister was fascinated. Josh loved to entertain. Jordan and I would climb in and sing silly songs and try to read books to her brother. Josh would get so excited by all the company though that it was hard for him to pay attention. The only time Jordan refused to enter is when it turned into a litter box. (Josh couldn't help but become relaxed in his cozy, private environment.) Of course, those were the times my husband vanished. I remember many days scrubbing and sanitizing and cussing my husband's creation.

"Jordan!" I would yell up. "Do you want to come in and help Mommy?"

If she could have, I'm sure she would have said, "Hell no!" But in her little, three-year-old voice, I'd hear her coo, "No thanks, Mommy, it's too stinky in there." She would just kindly lower all the organic cleaners and paper towels I needed to get the job done.

Soon we knew Josh was getting better and outgrowing his box. He had trained his body to sleep through the night. What a momentous, joyful day when, nine months after its construction, my husband finally dismantled it. I took only one picture.

It was an even better day when Josh graduated to his car bed. He loved crawling in and burrowing under the covers. He still does. We've been through several mattresses already, because Josh has to have at least twenty minutes of jump time before finally giving in to sleep. I'm proud to say that with diligence and great courage our son has made progress in all areas, and so have we.

Happily, we have more good days now than bad. There will always be a learning curve with autism; I know that. The future remains a question mark. But today our family has more tools, and I don't mean hooks 'n eyes and hammers, to deal with it. What a relief it is to slowly climb out of our own box and rejoin a world that's finally waking up to special kids like ours. For the first time in six years, the cup feels half full.

Shelley Stolaroff Segal

 Track Star

The track team accepted athletes based on their ability to run. Chase could run. He had been running all his life—running from the buzz in his head. If he ran enough, he could get away from the noise, that "say-so" following him, telling him what to do.

Here on the track, the pounding of his feet is louder than the buzz in his head. The sounds, the smell of sweat and dust, the focus on the long mile ahead leave the spinning of his mind back there somewhere.

Laugh now! Chase, smile at your mom with the camera. . . . Mom, mom, mom's hair.

"Mom, mom, mom's hair" is his name for me. Hair is one of his things. I am the mom thing.

Who was that shouting? . . . Coach.

"Six-ten, six-eleven. Come on. Chase! Six-twelve, -thirteen, -fourteen!" The coach swings his arm in a circle.

Thump, thump, thump. *The hair of the ponytail ahead . . . catch him. The hair of him . . . aaaaeeee! . . . hair.*

In the van, we pass groups of kids driving home from practice. Chase waves. The windows are open, and they turn to see who he is.

"Everyone knows me in Napa."

"Yes, Chase. That's right, Chase." Should I ask who they are?

At school he hangs out with his buddies in the quad. "I'm the fastest runner in the school, the fastest. I can run the mile in four minutes. I'm a track star."

"Cool, Chase! Way to go, Chase! Right on, Chase! See you at the track meet tomorrow!"

One kid clowning points to a student at the next table, a girl with a long black mane. "Hey, Chase, that girl likes you."

Chase leans over to touch the long strands. "Aaaeee." He pulls her hair gently up over her head. Her hair is the only part of her he can hold.

"Knock it off!" The girl moves away.

Chase laughs, getting up to leave. He is moving through the crowd, smiling, a bright marble bumping into other marbles rolling through a maze of colored book bags and T-shirts, faces talking and laughing, strands of black and blond hair floating. Cheerleaders group near the gym door.

"Hey, Chase! Good luck at the meet, Chase."

At home I watch from the front porch.

"Let's time you. Fifty yards start here." They've drawn a chalk line in the street. "Wait till I say go, Chase," his dad tells him.

"Ready. Set. Go!"

My husband, Dave, stands at the finish line looking in the direction of his son at the starting line. With his black jeans, tennis shoes, and baseball cap to protect his balding head, he looked loose, like, if he had to, he'd run himself. Beneath his trimmed and graying beard, he smiles. He's the kind of dad who does everything—volunteer coach, scout leader, fishing guide.

Jimmy, Chase's thirteen-year-old brother, watches from the starting line, arms crossed, waiting. Chase calls him "aaaeee hair." They have the same body type—athletic, long limbs, brown eyes and hair—but Chase's eyes look at you as though through something, a cloud, spots, fuzz. Jimmy's eyes see real things. A book is a book, a ball a ball. People are people.

Chase believes he is a track star—a high school track star. Dave punches the watch, swinging his arm down to the ground. "Six-seven. Great, Chase! Next time, run through the line. Don't stomp your feet."

I watch the angles of my son's body in motion, elbows, long legs bent, feet hitting hard . . . slap slap slap . . . the frustration and disgust paining his face. He quits running just before he hits the white line. Fear locks his legs. The ground holds his shoes.

"Let's try again, tiger." Dave pushes.

I interrupt, "Call it quits, already." Couldn't they see he was tired?

"Mom, go back inside." Jimmy says and walks back to the starting line. "Run with me and keep running through the end."

I watch both boys. One flies across the line, the other panics, halts, and then finally jumps over it.

Chase keeps working. Sweat drips off of him. He holds his arms out from his sides, palms up, pleading. "Ahhhhhhh! Do it again. It was five seconds . . . no, five seconds!"

"There's nothing wrong with the watch. It's six-seven." David is relentless.

I call to him from the porch. "It's okay, Chase. Come in the house now. Settle down. Take a shower. You did your best."

"It's five seconds. Five seconds! Five seconds!" His eyes widen.

Was I the only one who could see the confusion?

"I believe you. It was five seconds." It wasn't a real lie. It was a mom's lie.

Finally, I hear the shower running. So Chase can't hear me talking to Dave and Jimmy. "Can't you just lie, just agree with him?"

David was stubborn. "What? You want me to tell him he's a star, like everyone else does? He has to learn he's not the fastest. He'll learn."

Jimmy throws up his hands, "God, Mom. It's embarrassing. He acts like a baby!"

Round and round that same track, stubborn Dave, unsympathetic brother, Chase screaming. At meals, we talked about track times. In the car, we talked about the Olympics, about famous races, how much work it took to be a star.

"I am a track star, the fastest in high school."

"Sure, Chase. You're our star."

It was endless. Wasn't it easier to placate him, let him be happy, for God's sake? Big deal, if he says he's a track star. Who did it hurt? Why did they keep pushing to try to make him normal?

At the high school meets, Chase did the 400-meter, the 800-meter, and the mile. Sometimes he did the mile relay. The line didn't scare him on long runs, but he wouldn't sprint at the end. After each race, he told everyone—strangers, friends, and relatives—"Hello, my name is Chase." He'd flash a big grin. "I'm a track star."

At the next track meet, I sit on the bleachers, waiting for Coach Muela to give me instructions on how to time the runners. He needed parent volunteers, and I came to all the home meets at Vintage High. Coach, a slim man of medium build, wears a hat to keep the sun out of his eyes. A whistle hangs from his neck. He smiles at me with straight teeth below a mustache.

"We need second place and third. I've got first. Which one do you want?" He hands me a stopwatch.

"Second. I'll time second."

"Just wait to see smoke from the starting gun. When the second runner comes in, stop the watch. Find out the name of your runner and tell the girl at the table his time."

I look around for the girl at the table. A few yards away on the grass I spot a brown folding table, where a woman sits next to a young girl with a ponytail. "Okay, sounds easy. How's Chase doing?"

"Great. You know what I like about him? He does exactly what I tell him. He doesn't complain, like some of these kids: 'My ankle hurts,' or 'I'm too tired to run the next race.' Chase just runs when I tell him to run."

Chase walks up to us. "I'm varsity. Right, coach? I'm a varsity track star."

"You're my buddy, Chase, right? Don't wander off. Stay with me. I'll let you know when it's time for your run."

After a few junior races, it's time for Chase's mile. I take a break from the stopwatch, giving it to another parent. Chase stands at the starting line, his long legs bent, ready. He is lean and tall, five-eleven, and he has big feet, size eleven. His brown curly hair is unruly most of the time, and he doesn't like brushing it, so we keep it fairly short. His arms hang loose at his sides. Standing next to him are his two teammates; all three of their shirts are burgundy and say "VC," for Vintage Crushers, in gold letters. Two other teams wait too—Will C. Wood High in royal blue and yellow and Armijo in purple and white with a bold yellow A on the front of their jerseys. There are ten runners in all.

The gun goes off. Chase starts with a steady gait and keeps a steady rhythm. I love his smile, the way his body relaxes when he runs. Autism doesn't affect his body; if he could just get the time thing at the end.

"Go, Chase!" Did he hear me? Does he feel how the warm sun is browning his arms?

One of Wood's runners in blue shorts sprints past him, and then an Armijo boy is right with him for a cycle or two of their legs, but then he trots ahead, leaving Chase alone for a time. When he makes it round again, he is still smiling, still focused.

"Catch him, Chase!" someone yells from the crowd.

The last round, two more runners pull ahead, but Chase stays steady and smooth, a spoon stirring in liquid, despite Coach Muela yelling, "Pick it up, Chase!"

Kids shout from the bleachers. "Go, Chase! Come on, Chase! Get there, Chase!"

He doesn't listen. He stays fixed to the end and comes in ahead of two boys, both breathing heavy, sweating as they walk around trying to cool down. Chase doesn't look at me waving from the bleachers.

"Good race!" I call.

"What's my time?" Chase heads straight for Muela, wiping sweat from his forehead.

"Six-thirty-seven. Good job. Go stretch and get some water." Coach turns to follow other runners.

Chase trails him. "Four minutes, coach. Four minutes!"

Coach turns around. "We talked about that, buddy. It was six-thirty-seven. You've got to pick up your pace."

"I'm a track star, a varsity track star."

"Sure, buddy. You're a star, but Michael Johnson doesn't even run that fast!" Coach pats him on the back. "There's your mom, Chase. She helped today." He pointed to me.

I pick up my cooler containing extra water bottles and carry it over. I hand him one. "Go sit down and cool off."

Chase walks to the bleachers and sits down. I hear him tell one of the kids, "I run varsity. I'm a track star."

The kid smiles at Chase. I smile, because he kept running right to the end. This time, he finished almost last, but there will be more races. The kids who come in last learn the hardest lessons—how to run against the odds.

Barbara Toboni

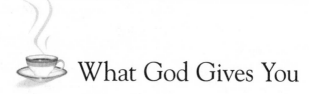

What God Gives You

W ant to know the two biggest lies people tell parents? "God never gives you more than you can handle," and "You must be an amazing parent, because God gave you a special child." When people repeat these sayings, I want to scream, "Bunk!" I can't believe God gives us difficult challenges just because we can handle them.

As anyone with a child on the autistic spectrum will tell you, it is life that throws us curveballs, not God. God is the one who gives us what we need to hit those curveballs out of the park.

Curveball No. 1: Foul Ball
My first child, Chris, appeared "typical" at birth. However, he had trouble falling asleep, easily became over-stimulated, and experienced meltdowns bordering on demonic possession. As my friends' kids didn't have these issues, I assumed that it was just my baby's personality. Little did I know his wild-child behavior would be the first of many parenting curveballs coming my way.

Curveball No. 2: A Double

While waiting in line to get an ultrasound for my second pregnancy, I overheard several women saying they were hoping for twins.

"You don't want twins," I told them. "My sister had twins, and even though she's Super Mom, she really struggled."

Want to guess who came out of the ultrasound room with news of multiples? I cried for days, sure I couldn't handle two at the same time. I was no Super Mom. As the news sunk in, I realized we needed a larger house and—gasp!—a minivan. House-shopping seven months pregnant with twins is not a pretty sight.

Then I had to deal with well-intentioned women patting my expanding belly and confiding stories of twin deliveries in which one died. Even the doctors and the books told me not to count on bringing both home. Now my thoughts of how in the world will I take care of two infants were replaced with not being able to bear the thought of filling only one of the two cribs in the nursery of our new home.

The twins' birth went surprisingly well, and neither my new baby boy nor his sister spent time in the neonatal intensive care unit. Still, I immediately felt overwhelmed by the two screaming infants in hospital basinets. I tried to send them to the nursery as often as possible, but the nurses kept bringing the babies back in my room, where the three of us howled together.

At home, family and friends pitched in for a while, and it wasn't until the twins were about six months old that I almost lost my mind (although I came close on a few sleepless nights early on). By then, all the help was gone, and I had returned to work in my in-home office. My husband often worked from morning until midnight for weeks at a time. Plus, my three-year-old let us know on a regular basis that he felt neglected, and his temper tantrums escalated. I knew without a doubt that I couldn't handle it all. Would I just start babbling uncontrollably one day?

Finally, I got daycare help and started to enjoy my babies and to feel as though I might have a handle on things. Until the twins turned two years old.

Curveball No. 3: Strike One

Around the twins' second birthday, people began commenting on how Mark, the boy twin, had become so shy. He stopped meeting people's eyes, preferred playing alone, and had stopped talking.

Up until then, he had developed typically. I knew this because of our built-in barometer—his twin, Sarah. They'd started crawling within a few weeks of each other, took their first steps a month apart, and began talking at the same time. But now it became obvious that Sarah had pulled ahead—way ahead.

Family members comforted me by saying that girls always developed quicker. Our pediatrician responded to my concerns about Mark's language loss with, "Wait and see. He'll probably start talking in full sentences."

But I could see him slipping further and further into his own world—a world that didn't include even his mother. So my husband and I took him to a specialist to rule out autism. Instead, the specialist confirmed our suspicions, and afterward we sat in our minivan, crying as if we would never stop. Cried for the little boy who would never know a typical life, and cried for our loss as well. Talking about it to others without more tears proved impossible, so I didn't. It became my secret burden.

At first, I hoped the diagnosis would someday change. Eventually, I accepted the truth. But accepting it didn't stop the pain. Crossing the street when a set of typical boy-girl twins approached kept me from seeing what might have been. The day he entered a special day preschool scorched my heart with the same agony as hearing the diagnosis.

My life became about newly-learned therapy acronyms as I rushed him to OT, PRT, DT, APE, and speech. And I began to worry about our totally typical Sarah being pushed into the background and left socially behind, as I didn't have time to go to play groups and playgrounds with her. Instead, she rode in the back of the van while I taxied Mark to his various therapies. Sometimes I just wanted to scream at the unfairness of it all: first twins and then autism!

Curveball No. 4: Change in the Lineup

But over the next three years, I could see my boy coming out of the haze of autism and slowly coming back to me. I will never forget the first time Mark called me "Mommy," at age three-and-a-half. Or when he said, "I love you," at four, something I wasn't sure I'd ever hear from him. Moments such as Mark standing up to his dominating twin aren't monumental for a typical kid, but with an autistic child they're cause for a party. I've learned to applaud even the tiniest of milestones.

After Mark's fifth birthday, he entered a typical preschool to catch up on socialization. By the end of the year, everyone agreed he could handle a typical classroom with an aide. A few weeks ago, Mark and Sarah began kindergarten together, just before their sixth birthday. Nothing in life has made me happier or prouder than the sight of them walking to class hand-in-hand, just like typical twins. Mark will always need extra coaching, but he's finally in the game.

Curveball No. 5: Strike Two

Big brother Chris's problems continued to become more pronounced. He struggled to finish schoolwork, to stay focused in the classroom, and to maintain friendships. At home, his ability to go emotionally from 0 to 80 in one second flat drained our family, while his loud voice continually assaulted our ears. I tried all my parenting tricks, read books to learn more, and even applied ABA (applied behavioral analysis) techniques that had worked well with Mark.

In second grade, Chris received an official diagnosis of ADHD. When I read that some doctors consider ADHD on the autistic spectrum, I took out the tissue box again and screamed in frustration, "Twins, autism, and now ADHD. I can't do this!"

After my tears dried, I found the right psychiatrist, tried Chris on new medications, and worked with the school to make him a more successful student. He still has far to go, but he's no longer striking out.

Seventh-Inning Stretch

People have asked my husband and me why we work so hard for our children. My answer is always the same: "Because we have no other choice." As philosopher and poet Rainer Maria Rilke said, "For one human being to love another human being, that is perhaps the most difficult task that has been entrusted to us, the ultimate task, the final test and proof, the work for which all other work is merely preparation."

I'm still not Super Mom, and I certainly don't deserve a halo. God didn't deem me so special that He gave me twins and made my boys special-needs. But He did give me strength when I couldn't hang on any longer; insight into my children, so I could help them; and inspiration when I needed it most.

There is a wonderful essay by Emily Pen Kingsley called "Welcome to Holland" in which she talks about planning a trip to Italy and ending up in Holland by accident. The smart traveler stops and enjoys all the amazing things Holland offers rather than regretting never making it to Italy. And that's what we finally did. As a result, we let all the small miracles in—miracles the parents of a typical child never experience.

Would I change Mark or Chris if I could wave a magic wand? In a heartbeat. What parent doesn't want their kids to have typical lives? But such magic doesn't exist; so instead I treasure a different kind of magic . . . the kind that is in my sons' every small victory and in every joyful moment with them and our daughter.

Life probably isn't through pitching me curveballs. In all honesty, I don't look forward to the next one, no matter how much richness the others have brought into my life. But I do know that when they come, I'll do my best to step up to the plate again. Not because I'm an amazing parent or chosen by God, but because I now know the playing field, and with God giving me what I need, I'll be able to go to bat and run the bases once more.

Patricia Morris Buckley

The children's names in this story have been changed to protect their privacy.

Beyond Survival

I knew I would be proud when he stepped off the bus, but I had no idea I would cry. I had seen him clear so many hurdles I hadn't expected I'd be moved to tears to witness another landmark. I tried to see inside the windows, squinting at the glare from the bright October sunlight. Would his face be a mask of tension and anxiety? *Would he be disconnected and distant, the experience of this trip undoing all the progress he had made?* I shivered as a sudden gust of wind blew down my neck, and wondered what the next minutes would reveal.

Four days earlier, after respecting Tanner's request not to hug him goodbye, I watched him board the bus with his fifth grade classmates, preparing to depart on a three-night field trip. He had always shied away from being touched; hugs, even in special situations, made him uncomfortable. I put on a brave face, but inside I was a writhing bundle of anxiety.

With a tickle of horror, I mentally listed some of the compulsions that could interfere with his ability to have fun: obsessing over the seams of his socks to the point of tears of despair if they did not lie straight inside his shoes; his aversion to the sound of his nylon rain poncho, preferring to strip it off in a downpour rather than endure the assault on his senses. On this trip, he would be meeting new adults and new peers—people who did not know him, who might not understand.

We had always sensed something was different about our son. From the time he was a toddler, he could smile, laugh, answer questions, and converse awkwardly. Still, he seemed only partially present in the world.

I vividly remember how he greeted any visitor who rang our doorbell with the same words each time, spoken in a tiny, stilted voice that lacked any emotion: "Oh, hi. It's you. Come on in." The greeting never varied. When those same visitors replied with a happy hello, he stared into space like a wax statue, offering no reply . . . or simply walked away. He had responded to the sound of the doorbell, but not to the human being who pressed it! I was chagrined by his seeming inability to learn even simple manners. He did, however, possess a keen intellect.

"He must be a genius!" we bragged. "Only three, and he can write his full name! He counted to thirty at eighteen months old! At twenty-four months, he was using the computer!"

Secretly, though, we worried. He was obsessive about certain things. He would say the same sentence or draw the same picture over and over again. Once, at age four, he spent three uninterrupted hours quietly drawing fifty-seven African masks, giving them titles that sounded oddly lyrical: the State Monkey Mask, the Jupiter Mask, the Night Thunder Mask. We were disturbed by a variety of behaviors that seemed odd, unreasonable, or downright unnatural. His shrieking in horror if we dressed him in a fleecy sweatshirt, trying to tear it off as though he were on fire. Covering his ears for periods of time and humming in a quiet, atonal drone. His speech limited to only direct quotes from movies and commercials. I longed to know my child. A wall was between us; we could see each other, yet we could not reach each other. To understand our child, we knew we had to look deeper.

The summer before Tanner turned five, I began an earnest search for answers. That autumn, he would enter kindergarten. I knew a formal diagnosis would give him access to more targeted support services through the school. I began reading everything I could find on learning disabilities. I looked into disabilities ranging from nonverbal learning disorder to audio-processing issues, but nothing fit.

As fall turned into winter, Tanner began having some struggles in school—hiding under his desk, covering his ears when distressed, refusing to speak when spoken to. The school did their best to offer him time to transition and a quiet spot for regrouping when his senses were overwhelmed. Were we destined to address one puzzling behavior at a time, finding solutions through trial and error?

Then one grey February day, my mother e-mailed me an article from *Wired* magazine called "The Geek Syndrome." As I read through the opening paragraph, I felt a knot form in my throat. It described a young boy with a form of autism. As I read further into the story, the knot slowly untied itself and tears spilled down my cheeks. At last, I had found the name of the disorder that colored my son's life in such unusual ways: Asperger's syndrome.

I quickly made an online purchase of four books on Asperger's and autism, including *How to Eat an Artichoke* by Echo Fling, and *Asperger's Syndrome: A Guide for Parents and Professionals* by Tony Attwood. I read each one with a sense of hope and relief. I noted which professionals I could consult to confirm my discovery and set about making appointments.

Our visit a few weeks later with Dr. Boone, our pediatrician, left me feeling angry and inadequate.

"I believe he has Asperger's syndrome," I announced with conviction. Dr. Boone raised his eyebrows questioningly. "It is a mild form of autism," I added, with less certainty this time.

Now he regarded me with slight alarm. "I have never even heard of it." he proclaimed. He turned to my son, and asked him, "What is your name?"

"Tanner," my son replied.

"Do you like ice cream?" the doctor continued.

"Yes."

Dr. Boone turned back to me, satisfied with this brief exchange. "There is nothing wrong with him. He has social skills, and he makes eye contact. Truly autistic children don't talk when spoken to."

His ignorance hit me harder than any slap; what a shock to catch a doctor in the act of being absolutely wrong! I took out a pen and notebook, and shaking a bit, jotted down the titles of the books I had read so voraciously. I had never disagreed with an authority figure before, certainly not a doctor.

With my heart climbing up the walls of my chest, I handed him the list and said, my voice a bit unsteady, "I think you are wrong. Tanner needs to see a specialist. You do the children in this practice a disservice when you don't take the time to recognize what is in front of you." On shaking legs, my son in tow, I left the office.

Two days later, Dr. Boone's office called. An appointment had been arranged for us with a pediatric neurologist. I felt triumphant. It was not an apology, but it felt pretty close.

The road to diagnosis can be a long one. It can be marked by offshoots, dead-ends, and unblazed trails. Well-meaning onlookers share articles about medications, supplements, genetics, diet, vaccinations, and prayer. That spring, the appointments with the pediatric neurologist resulted in a formal diagnosis of Asperger's syndrome, as I had suspected. Though I felt relief in knowing we had a medical term for the behaviors Tanner exhibited, I also experienced deep anguish. I knew this was only the beginning of our journey. What if I were not up to the job of mothering this wonderful, unusual boy? Surely some sort of expertise was required? I could barely keep up with the demands of my daily routine; our family had grown over the years, and Tanner had two little brothers who also needed me.

Tanner's school became a source of great support. He was the first child they had with such a diagnosis, and they were eager to learn more about it. So his teachers and I learned together. Through first, second, and third grades, the Individualized Education Program (IEP) we designed for him seemed to offer the support he needed—a weekly social skills group, visits to the social worker when he was distressed, extra time on tests. I watched my son closely through these years to see how he was faring in a world not aligned with his own, praying that world would be kind.

Despite the success of those years, there was a distinct change the year he entered fourth grade. At eight years old, he suddenly found himself in uncharted territory. We watched with dismay as he floundered in a rough social and academic sea he was not neurologically built for. Classmates teased, teachers grew exasperated with lost assignments and inattentiveness, his grades plummeted, and his anxiety grew, sending him deeper into his shell.

"His behavior is willful and manipulative," his teacher announced, citing his lack of cooperation.

I understood her frustration, but I knew he was not choosing these behaviors. Rather, Tanner was trying desperately to protect himself. Complex social situations left him bewildered and panic-stricken, eclipsing his ability to concentrate. He had trouble understanding sarcasm, struggled to read facial expressions, and could not keep up with quick-moving conversations. His anxiety was so consuming that he retreated to a solitary place in his mind. There, the pain could not reach him, but neither could the voices of those who tried to help him.

The social, physical, and academic challenges of Asperger's had lurked beneath the surface like an iceberg, and his little vessel had struck it hard. He was truly drowning. In the early spring, we sought the help of a child psychiatrist.

After meeting with us, the psychiatrist suggested Tanner try Abilify, a medication designed for bi-polar disorders but used off-label for social anxiety. Our concerns outweighed our reservations. Clearly, we needed to take strong measures. The reality that unfolded within days was profound.

"How was your day, Mom?" he asked when I picked him up from school eight days after his first dose.

My mouth gaped in astonishment. I had no ready answer; he had never been moved to ask this before!

"Hi, Mrs. Ruskin," he called to our neighbor as we walked by.

She, too, looked at him in amazement. He had never spoken directly to her in the five years we had been neighbors. Over a four-week period, I watched in grateful disbelief as my son emerged, piece by beautiful piece, from the safety of his rigid exterior. He looked people in the eye and answered them when spoken to. He smiled and joked more. He was patient with his siblings, and, to my absolute joy, returned hugs. His grades climbed, his confidence soared, his tantrums abated. Our whole family was vibrantly transformed by these new connections with Tanner. I realized that for the first time in our lives, we were meeting our son. Free from much of his anxiety, Tanner passed through the window from his world to ours. Even today, nine months later, I am transfixed with wonder at seemingly small gestures of affection and understanding from him; to us, they are enormous and profound.

Still, when Tanner insisted on going on his class field trip, I was impressed but concerned.

"How will I survive?" I teased. "I will miss you too much!"

He rolled his eyes good-naturedly. "Mom, I will miss you, too, but I think I'm going to have fun." I had to honor his confidence and send him in good faith.

Yes, I knew I would be proud when he came off that bus. He had coped several days with new people, rules, routines, and environments. Yet, what brought on my tears as he stepped off the bus was seeing his face—his shining eyes looking directly into mine as he grinned ear-to-ear, before running to me and engulfing me in a tight embrace, proclaiming with a laugh, "Hey, Mom! We did it! We survived!"

Nicole Derosier

Martha Stewart Doesn't Live Here

I used to be one of those people you could almost hate. I had floors so clean you could eat off of them and a 50- by 100-foot organic garden. I'd can fifty quarts of tomato sauce in one night and grind my own wheat. Back off!—I own a butter churn, and I know how to use it! I also had clean closets and a savings account that didn't echo, and I donated items we'd outgrown to charity in a timely manner. In other words, I was completely neurotic.

Then our oldest son was diagnosed with Asperger's syndrome . . . then our second son . . . and eventually our daughter. Overnight, our lives went from a quiet life on the farm to driving constantly in the car. We live 30 miles from the city, so it's a shame they don't give frequent flyer miles for trips on the freeway. The intensity of focus changed from living a life that looked like perfection to seeking out the elusive perfect solution to our child's neurological disorder through outside intervention. I won't list the multitude of therapists, doctors, and practitioners we visited that first year; suffice to say they were numerous. And expensive. Savings depleted, we said, "Do you take Visa?"

Initially, we dragged our two younger kids along to their brother's appointments of parental desperation merely for the joyous experience of spending endless hours with young children in waiting rooms. There are only so many means of entertainment and distraction that parents can stuff in their backpacks. Funny how these appointments seemed to often end at noon. Juice boxes and PB&J get old fast. But no worries, there's a McDonalds on the way home.

Eighteen months, $17,000, and a 25-pound weight gain (that would be me) later, we took a look around and said, "This doesn't seem to be working." We began to make changes. However, we did not go back to the way things had been before—because, not only was that impossible, we also didn't want to.

Looking back to before the day we refer to as "The Diagnosis," I now clearly see the need I'd had to control our environment in my attempt to be Super Homemaker. Having difficult, sensitive kids tends to make life chaotic. Social engagements were largely disastrous. Outings with our children often resulted in meltdowns, and I felt I was being judged by others over my seeming failure as a mom. Well-intentioned but misguided "suggestions" by others led to further self-criticism on my part. As the situation worsened, our family withdrew and became isolated in a self-protective cocoon. At the time, I was doing the only thing I knew how to do to manage both the kids' symptoms and my anxiety: I ran from my niggling doubts and feelings of helplessness by hiding out in our well-scrubbed home. I was operating on the false belief that if only I could be a perfect mom and have a perfect home, then my kids would be, well, maybe not perfect, but okay. Everything would be all right if I just tried hard enough.

After The Diagnosis, we turned to professionals, because we were "only" parents and desperately needed answers. We felt helpless, worried, and frightened by the word autism. Though we didn't admit it, we were still operating on a misguided notion that maybe we could "fix" what was wrong with our child. We were so fearful of the unknown that we threw ourselves into focusing completely on treatments and tried not to think about the future. Again, this stemmed from our irrational belief that everything might be all right if we just tried hard enough. Maybe if we do just this one more thing . . . .

Some of these treatments were a waste of money, time, and energy. I'll never forget one particular alternative practitioner. As I wrote out the check after the treatment, he proceeded to share his belief that children with autism were, in fact, angels/aliens. Later he informed me that during treatment he'd been telling my son (telepathically, thankfully), "Welcome to Earth!" Then there was the doctor who insisted we order an herbal remedy, which cost us hundreds of dollars and ultimately reaped the sole result of making our son bounce off the walls even more than usual.

Of course, not all the treatments were bogus. In fact, most of those we tried were legitimate and brought positive, if not always the hoped-for, results. It's just that there were so many of them, and we lost sight of what we were trying to accomplish as we chased this elusive goal from one appointment to another.

I finally took a hard look at our family life and asked myself, *Is it really helpful to expend all of my energy on making our home so spotless it looks as though no one lives here? And while we have found therapies that do improve the lives of our children, is it really beneficial to drag them all over kingdom come with no time to relax and merely enjoy being children? My poor harried husband and bedraggled kids! Not to mention that I wasn't feeling much joy in life either. There had to be a better answer.*

It has taken time, but eventually we struck some balance. Instead of seeking perfection in our home and a cure for our kids, we've settled on embracing the imperfections in both.

In recent years I've learned a few things about homemaking that Martha Stewart will never tell you, but they have served me well.

It doesn't matter if there are always dishes in the sink or laundry in the basket (or even better, piled in the chair in the family room). My kids do not notice or care, just as long as they are fed and clothed. They would rather eat macaroni and cheese out of a box than to have me make it from organic whole grain spelt and three types of hand-grated organic cheeses. In fact, if I make the latter, they'll gag, I'll get frustrated, and dinnertime will be shot anyway, so I'm better off sticking with the box. It doesn't matter if there is a half empty (possibly moldy) jar of spaghetti sauce in the back of the fridge, as long as it doesn't smell bad. I don't need to move my sofa to vacuum; in fact, I don't ever have to look under there at all . . . again, unless something smells. Then and only then is it necessary to investigate.

We've embraced the homemaking goal of "clean enough to be healthy, dirty enough to be happy." Grandma might have called this giving the house "a lick and a promise," but it frees up loads of time to do something rare and precious—enjoy life with our children.

I still bake bread now and then, but the wheat grinder is buried somewhere in the back of the cupboard. Now, the process usually involves sticky-fingered children helping me pour cups of store-bought flour into the bread maker. Guess what? It tastes almost the same!

Our home is still a cozy cocoon, but we manage to leave it on occasion to risk the social consequences.

We brave the cruel world, knowing we will be judged on occasion, but we care less about what others might think. We understand why our children behave as they do and acknowledge we are doing the best we can, which is all we can expect from ourselves. We are bolstered by the community of support we've built of families like ours, who understand the struggles we face and suffer the same painful doubts about their parenting (despite the fact that they are fabulous parents). But we've also been surprised to learn that, although not everyone has kids like ours (and especially not three of them), most people are kinder than we tend to give them credit for. Everyone has challenges in their lives; when we share ours, they usually respond with compassion and the same desire for acceptance that we all wish for.

On the therapy front, we've found things that help our children. We have a core group of professionals who understand our children's needs and make an enormous difference We depend on their expertise and are extremely grateful to them. They never say the word "cure," which helps our level of trust. We no longer run around frantically in a panic, so afraid of our children's adulthood that we make ourselves and them nutty. Instead, we focus on attainable goals for the short-term, with a realistic but optimistic eye turned toward the future. We are aware of other therapies that might be beneficial—in fact, some are highly recommended and considered effective treatments for children with autism. But, after weighing out the time, money, and effort involved, we decided that, at least for now, we will not pursue these things. Do we sometimes have doubts about that choice? Yes. But we also keep in mind those days when we were flying up and down the freeway, burning up all our resources, time, and energy, and how miserable our children (and we) were. So, instead, we settle on a few treatments that we have found helpful and spend much of our former freeway time taking walks with the kids or reading to them.

Significant changes have led to our finding a better balance. Perhaps the most significant change for us is that, because we've stopped looking to fix our family, we've been able to see and embrace our unique-ness, our special gifts, and to recognize what amazing children we have. Yes, our children are challenging, but they are also loving, caring human beings who embrace life in a way that we could all learn from.

Nothing is perfect, and we accept "good enough." Our life now reflects our children's true needs. We take care of the basic necessities at home. We seek out help and support in the community. And we give ourselves the gift of being grateful for the blessings we have. It works for us. We are an Asperger's syndrome family, but first and foremost, we are simply a family.

Kristi Sakai

Oh, the Things I Say

"Nicky, I told you to take the magic out of your pocket. Now it's all over the washing machine!"

One afternoon, I actually found those words coming out of my mouth. The "magic" was sequin-like confetti, and the water had plastered it to the inside of the washing machine. When I'd held my first baby in my arms seven years earlier, I'd never imagined saying something like that.

Of course, that's nothing compared to the things I say to his younger brother. Things like, "Kyle, don't bang your head on the glass," and "Kyle, don't stand on the TV," and "Kyle, say, 'I love you, Mommy.'"

I hadn't anticipated needing to install the alarm system (complete with a clear plastic lockbox over the control pad), or the door pins and chains, or the thumb-screw window locks that would cause most rational people to wonder why we're so paranoid. Then again, when I'd rocked my little Kyle to sleep five years before, I couldn't have imagined a child who would kick out the window screens and dash outside in his underwear.

I hadn't expected a lot of things that came with being a mom, including Kyle's diagnosis of autism. His big brother, Nicky, not only developed normally, he also reached all his childhood milestones early—walking at nine months and speaking so well by the age of three that people did double-takes at the things he said. How could we ever have suspected that Kyle would be so different? There was no warning, not a single diagnosed case of autism in the family.

Of course, we had heard of autism but knew little about it. Our only clues had come from extreme-case tales of autistic savants and movies such as *Rain Man*, depicting autism as a rare condition that means life in a long-term care facility. It was a tremendous shock to learn that 1 in 160 children in the United States are diagnosed with autism, which, we also learned, is not one specific set of symptoms but, rather, encompasses a broad spectrum of disorders ranging from high-functioning to severely disabled. Many of those on the autism spectrum, if given proper therapy and education, will go on to lead typical—and sometimes even exceptional—lives. How could there be such a staggering number of people with autism and so little common knowledge about it?

I recalled running into one of my former teachers and his son at the grocery store a few months before we received my son's diagnosis. What I had mistaken for shyness in his child had, in fact, been autism. The symptoms were right there in front of me, and I hadn't recognized them, wouldn't even have guessed at the time.

Unfortunately, I'm far from being alone in missing the signs. It's not hard to do. Many forms of autism include lack of eye contact and poor to no language skills, which people often misread as shyness. In children with autism, frustration from the inability to communicate, the desire to have basic needs met, or difficulty understanding and coping with change often manifests as a tantrum—another behavior that is frequently misunderstood.

One evening last summer, Kyle and I stood in a slow-moving line for ice cream at a crowded Disney park. Everyone was hot and annoyed by the delay, exchanging impatient glances and comments. Kyle asked, "Ready, set, go?"—which meant he wanted to move forward to the ice cream stand. It didn't happen, and before long, his normally sweet little voice was shrill. "Treat! Ready, set, go!" I held his hand tightly as the jumping began. Then came the screaming, the hitting, and the head-banging on my arm.

The man in line behind me tried to be kind and cheer Kyle up a bit. "You're at Disney World. You should be happy." He asked Kyle if he'd seen Mickey Mouse.

"He won't answer you," I said.

Thinking he understood, the man said, "Yeah, he's only got one thing on his mind right now."

Eventually, the line crept forward. Kyle finally got his ice pop and calmed down.

"All better?" I asked him.

"All better?" he repeated.

The man smiled and said to Kyle, "You sure are spoiled."

At the time, the remark caught me off-guard, and I said nothing. It bothered me, though, how people jump to conclusions about my son, about autistic behavior in general, just as I had done with my teacher's son. Because people can't see autism the way they see a wheelchair, they assume that a quiet child is shy, that a tantrum means the parents can't control their kid.

In a sense, they're right about that much—I can't control Kyle, because he can't control himself. So instead, I've found my voice. I say things like, "He's not spoiled; he's autistic." I turn people's stares into teaching opportunities with T-shirts bearing the message: *Quiet doesn't always mean shy. A tantrum doesn't always mean naughty. AUTISM—Would you know it if you saw it?* I also hand out printed cards explaining that my child is autistic and that behavior they may consider rude is often his only way of dealing with the world around him.

Sometimes, the people say nothing; sometimes, they react with sympathy. Either way, I speak out, and on occasion I'm still surprised at the things I say.

I went to a local jeweler to order a puzzle-piece charm. During our conversation, I told him the piece represented autism and that I had an autistic son.

I returned to pick up the charm a few days later. Kyle was with me and determined to get into all the cases filled with sparkling gold and silver, twinkling diamonds, and colorful semi-precious stones. As I struggled to keep the little guy out of mischief, I said to the jeweler, "This is the son I mentioned."

He looked at Kyle with a kind of sadness in his eyes and then shook his head. "What a tragedy."

I looked down at the beautiful child sitting at my feet, at his dimpled smile, at his big blue eyes alight with joy at the sight of so many glittering things in one place, listened to his happy giggle, and raised my eyebrows. Years ago, I never imagined I'd complain about magic in the washing machine. I certainly never dreamed that I'd smile at my own autistic son and reply, "Tragedy? No, not really. The only tragedy would be in not having him."

D. M. Rosner

Contributors

Christina Adams ("Flying"), M.F.A., is the author of *A Real Boy: A True Story of Autism, Early Intervention and Recovery*. She has written for National Public Radio, the *Los Angeles Times Magazine*, *The Los Angeles Times*, and *Brain Child Magazine*. She also speaks to national audiences on creative writing, early intervention, the autism spectrum and education.

Judy L. Adourian ("A Vehicle of Change") is a freelance writer in Coventry, Rhode Island. She is the owner of Writ-eyes, a teaching, critiquing, and support network for writers. She is also the executive editor for *NEWN* magazine and a member of the International Women's Writing Guild. This is her third publication in the *Cup of Comfort* book series.

Deborah Barrett-Jardine ("Dancing with Puddles") holds a PhD in clinical psychology and has been a psychotherapist for over fifteen years. She lives with her son, Anthony, and husband, David, in Edmonton, Alberta, Canada. Deborah is fascinated by transformation and spiritual growth as it happens in the lives of ordinary people.

Amy Baskin ("A Child Slips the Bonds of Earth") is an author and speaker in Guelph, Ontario, Canada. Her work appears in magazines throughout North America. She co-authored the book *More Than a Mom: Living a Full and Balanced Life When Your Child Has Special Needs*.

Lorri Benedik ("The Singing Blues") was born and raised in Montreal, Canada. She lives in the suburbs with her humorous husband, Manny, their sweet, sensitive son, Zach, and beloved dog, Beauty. Music continues to be a big part of their lives—these days, mostly hip hop, rock, and rap.

Patricia Morris Buckley ("What God Gives You") is an award-winning journalist with twenty-three years of experience. Her work has appeared in the *Los Angeles Times, Alaska Airlines Magazine, Dog Fancy*, and many other national publications. Her children's writing has been printed in several national magazines. She is currently working on a children's book about autism.

Thomas Cannon ("Part of the Gift") is a special education teacher for school-aged children at a mental health facility. Thomas and his wife, Linda, live in Oshkosh, Wisconsin, with their two daughters and their youngest child, whom this story is about. They believe intensive, in-home therapy is crucial for children with autism.

Jennifer Casey ("Learning to Talk") lives near London, England. She shares her home with a small menagerie of pets and three children, two of whom are on the autistic spectrum. She currently runs a small child care business specifically for children with disabilities. In her spare time, she writes poetry.

Anne Clark ("Lunar Eclipse") lives with her family in the San Francisco Bay Area. She is using a pseudonym to honor her son's wishes.

Nicole Derosier ("Beyond Survival") is married to her college sweetheart and is mother of their three busy, happy boys. When not slaying daily domestic dragons, she can be found in her art studio, creating paintings and mixed-media works. On days when she feels life is pulling her under, she remembers her sense of humor can be used as an emergency floating device.

Karen Doyle ("The Weird Kid") is a full-time financial planner and part-time freelance writer. She has written for corporate clients, public relations firms, and parenting publications. A recovering housewife, she lives in Scituate,

Massachusetts, with her husband and three children, who provide her with endless subject matter for her humor writing.

Penelope Feeny ("To Welcome Chance") is a freelance writer who has also worked as an editor, broadcaster, and arts administrator. She was born in Cambridge (U.K.) and lived in London and Rome before settling in Liverpool, England. She is married to a lawyer, and they have five wonderful children, the youngest of whom has severe learning difficulties and autism.

Elizabeth King Gerlach ("Cake and Polyester Don't Mix") is Nick's mother. She is the author of two award-winning books, *Autism Treatment Guide* and *Just This Side of Normal: Glimpses into Life with Autism* (Future Horizons). She lives in Oregon.

Jenan Gray ("Portrait of a Princess") is a psychiatric nurse-therapist turned college student and an at-home mom who lives in the Tampa Bay Area. In between Boy Scouts, hurricanes, and final exams, she is writing her first novel, a political murder mystery.

Lauren Finaldi Gürus ("A Is for Ability"), a Chicago native who currently resides in Florida, is a poet, artist, wife, and mother of Erin, Rachel, and Alp (all eleven years old). Her poetry has been published in several online literary magazines, including The *Centrifugal Eye, Poems Neiderngasse,* and *Flashquake.* Her stepson, Alp, who has autism and Tourette syndrome, has been not only her greatest life challenge but also a great source of inspiration.

Kelly Harland ("Escalatorland" and "Moonlight") is a singer, writer, and voice teacher living in Seattle. She is on the faculty of Cornish College of the Arts and is a recording artist with two CDs on the jazz label Origin. Her book of essays about her son, *A Will of His Own,* is in its second printing.

Kathryn Hutchinson ("Leaving Literalville") is a life-long resident of northwest suburban Chicago. She has taught

English for twenty years at a large high school, where she also serves as the fine and performing arts coordinator. Kate is an arts aficionado, avid reader, and student of Eastern philosophy. Ramon is her only child.

Nan Jacobs ("Word Games") resides in Pennsylvania with her self-employed husband, son, granny, two cats, five bunnies, three hermit crabs, and eight tow trucks. When not dispatching tow trucks, she writes fiction, humorous essays, and relaxes with episodes of *Due South*. She and her son each have had several poems published in the anthology *Tides of the Heart*.

Heather Jensen ("Because We Were Prepared" and "What Comes Next?") is a poet and freelance writer, living in Cheyenne, Wyoming. Her goals include the completion of a novel and publication of a nonfiction memoir. She shares her heart and home with a loving, supportive husband, three children, and two freeloading cats.

F. L. Justice ("A Child Like Me") lives in Brooklyn, New York, where she writes historical novels. She is also self-diagnosed with Asperger's syndrome and has co-founded a parents' support group in Manhattan. G. L. Stein is still pursuing his passion for journalism, working for CBS as a producer. Anna is now fifteen and thinking about college.

Jason Katims ("The Pray Grounds") is a writer/producer who has worked on the television shows *My So-Called Life* and *Boston Public* and created the shows *Roswell* and *Relativity*. He also co-wrote the movie *The Pallbearer* and has written numerous plays. He lives in Los Angeles with his wife Kathy and children, Sawyer and Phoebe.

Angie Lathrop ("Entomology"), a small-animal veterinarian, lives on a farm in south central Wisconsin with her husband, Alan Treinen, and sons Thomas and Patrick. Thomas is on the autism spectrum. Angie also manages and promotes their corn maze and pumpkin patch business, in addition to writing fiction and nonfiction.

Dena Fox Luchsinger ("How the Goose Saved Christmas") is a writer and the mother of three children, one of whom has the dual diagnosis of Down's syndrome and autism. She is the author of *The Babysitter*, a children's book featuring an autistic child and his sister (Woodbine House). She lives with her family in Wasilla, Alaska.

Shawn Daywalt Lutz ("The Head in the Head") lives in Capistrano Beach, California, and is a happily married mother of two. She enjoys volunteering at her children's school and singing in the church choir. She has worked as an actress, singer, and voice-over artist, but now enjoys channeling her creating spirit into writing.

Phyllis Mannan ("Pot Roast Coming Around the Clock") lives with her husband in Portland, Oregon, and substitute teaches high school English and special education classes. She enjoys spending time with her family on the Oregon coast. Her poems have been published in several Northwest literary journals. Her son David, who has autism, is the oldest of three children.

Katherine Millett ("Getting Along") is the freelance writer of dozens of published articles. She writes about musicians, doctors, mountain climbers, prisoners, cities, and wilderness. A recovering lawyer, she lives in Elmhurst, Illinois, with her husband and their two sons.

Michelle O'Neil ("An Exercise in Acceptance") is a registered nurse and a former radio news reporter. She currently lives in Lynchburg, Virginia, with her husband and two young children. Her daughter is thriving under the care of a DAN! (Defeat Autism Now!) physician, who is using bio-medical approaches to treat her sensory integration disorder.

Suzanne M. Perryman ("Sara's First Friend") is the publisher of *Embroidery Journal*. She is a passionate, advocating mother of two girls, a community volunteer for Raising Special Kids–Arizona, and president of the Arizona chapter of the

United Mitochondrial Disease Foundation. She and her daughters reside in Scottsdale, Arizona, with her husband, Bruce.

Caroline M. Praed ("Between the Lines") and her family live just south of London, England. She is homeschooling her daughter, who has almost finished writing her fourth novel. Tim finished writing his first story last summer. The three are in competition to be the first to get a book published.

Sonja Predovich ("Confessions of a Mortal Mom") lives in Colorado with her husband and three children. She is both a stay-at-home-mom and an online college student, pursuing a master's degree in special education. Her experience in the world of autism, while challenging, has awakened a passion in her for children who don't fit with traditional schools. It has helped her to find her voice and perhaps her life calling.

D. M. Rosner ("Oh, the Things I Say") is a published author of fiction and nonfiction. In response to the widespread misunderstanding of autism, she started Autism Gear, a Web-based business offering a variety of awareness items, many of which she designs herself. She lives with her husband and two sons in central Florida.

Kristi Sakai ("Martha Stewart Doesn't Live Here") lives on a farm in Oregon with her husband, Nobuo, and their three children, Tom, Kito, and Kaede, all of whom have Asperger's syndrome. She is the author of *Finding Our Way: Practical Solutions for Creating a Supportive Home and Community for the Asperger's Syndrome Family*.

Rebekah Schow ("The Offering"), who lives in the Intermountain West, has devoted her life to homemaking while pursuing a variety of interests. She has successfully written for children and teens and enjoys photography and four-wheeling with her family in the mountains and forests near her home. Rebekah holds a master's degree in mental health counseling.

Christy Shoemaker ("Blazing New Trails") is a some-times-teacher, sometimes-writer, sometimes-runner, and always-mother living with her family in Boulder, Colorado. She is both inspired and humbled by the other parents she has met on her journey, starting with "the magazine dad." She is enjoying the joy-filled years of experience with her son more than she ever thought possible.

Kristen M. Scott ("Good Marching") lives in Deerfield, Illinois, with her husband and two children. A part-time church administrator, she leads a support group for parents of children with special needs, focusing on the emotional impact of parenting extraordinary children. Her essays have appeared in the online journal *Mom Writers Literary Magazine*, *The Chicago Tribune*, and the weekly suburban papers of the Pioneer Press.

Shelley Stolaroff Segal ("Outside Inside the Box") is a writer, composer, and performer living in Greensboro, North Carolina. After earning a degree in English literature at University of North Carolina-Chapel Hill, she received her theatrical training at the Drama Studio, in London, England. She is married to Dr. Jeffrey Segal, a neurosurgeon and currently an autism researcher. She was recently published in the anthology *Voices from the Spectrum*.

Piper Selden ("Snake Dreams") is a writer, artist, and mother of a special needs child. She lives on the Big Island of Hawaii with her two children, husband, and geriatric cat. Her writing includes fiction, nonfiction, and poetry. Piper's work as an environmental educator inspired her latest book, *Composting for Couch Potatoes*.

Jill W. Smith ("Searching for Normal") is a writer living in Burnsville, Minnesota, with her husband and two daughters. She is a degree candidate in the Master of Fine Arts program at Hamline University. When not pursuing a literary

A Cup of Comfort for Parents of Children with Autism ～ 319

career, most recently writing a memoir, she writes professionally for a children's health organization in St. Paul.

Tiffany Talbott ("Arms Wide Open") is a writer and photographer based in Portland, Oregon, where she lives with her husband and son. She is currently working on a novel and is coeditor of the e-zine *Thereby Hangs a Tale*.

Tabitha Thompson ("Sophie's Song") is a freelance writer in Park City, Utah. She is working on a nonfiction book about Patricia, Sophie, and the community center Patricia founded for families affected by autism. Tabitha has been editor at *Utah Business* and *WHERE Phoenix/Scottsdale* magazines, and her work has appeared in numerous regional and national publications, including *Orion Online*.

Barbara Toboni ("Track Star") lives in Napa, California, where she and her husband run a computer business. She earned her A.A. degree from the Napa Valley College in 2003. She is currently working on a collection of stories about raising her autistic son, who is now an adult.

Jennifer Finn Wake ("Brothers") lives in Walnut Creek, California, with her husband, Dan, and their two sons. A freelance writer whose work has appeared in magazines and newspapers, Jennifer keeps busy with occasional speaking engagements and drawing caricatures at local fundraising events, and is currently working on her third novel.

James C. Wilson ("Life with the Family Gangsta") lives in West Chester, Ohio, and teaches at the University of Cincinnati. He has written about his son Sam in *Mothering* and *Exceptional Parent* magazines as well as in the anthology *Uncommon Fathers*. His last book, which he edited with Cynthia Lewiecki-Wilson, is *Embodied Rhetorics: Disability in Language and Culture*.

Tell Your Story in the Next *Cup of Comfort*!

We hope you have enjoyed *A Cup of Comfort for Parents of Children with Autism* and that you will share it with all the special people in your life.

You won't want to miss our next heartwarming volumes, *A Cup of Comfort for Writers* and *A Cup of Comfort for Dog Lovers*. Look for these new books in your favorite bookstores soon!

We're brewing up lots of other *Cup of Comfort* books, each filled to the brim with true stories that will touch your heart and soothe your soul. The inspiring tales included in these collections are written by everyday men and women, and we would love to include one of your stories in an upcoming edition of *A Cup of Comfort*.

Do you have a powerful story about an experience that dramatically changed or enhanced your life? A compelling story that can stir our emotions, make us think, and bring us hope? An inspiring story that reveals lessons of humility within a vividly told tale? Tell us your story!

Each *Cup of Comfort* contributor will receive a monetary fee, author credit, and a complimentary copy of the book. Just e-mail your submission of 1,000 to 2,000 words (one story per e-mail; no attachments, please) to:

cupofcomfort@adamsmedia.com

Or, if e-mail is unavailable to you, send it to:

A Cup of Comfort
Adams Media
57 Littlefield Street
Avon, MA 02322

You can submit as many stories as you'd like, for whichever volumes you'd like. Make sure to include your name, address, and other contact information and indicate for which volume you'd like your story to be considered. We also welcome your suggestions or stories for new *Cup of Comfort* themes.

For more information, please visit our Web site: *www.cupofcomfort.com.*

We look forward to sharing many more soothing *Cups of Comfort* with you!

About the Editor

Colleen Sell is the editor of sixteen volumes of the *Cup of Comfort* anthology series. She has been a book author, editor, and ghostwriter as well as a magazine editor, journalist, technical writer, and copywriter. She and her husband, T. N. Trudeau, share a big old farmhouse, which they are perpetually renovating, on forty wild acres, which they are slowly turning into an organic lavender, blueberry, holly, and pumpkin farm in the magnificent Pacific Northwest.

The *Cup of Comfort* Series!

All titles are $9.95 unless otherwise noted.

A Cup of Comfort
1-58062-524-X

A Cup of Comfort Devotional ($12.95)
1-59337-090-3

A Cup of Comfort Devotional for Mothers ($12.95)
1-59869-152-X

A Cup of Comfort Devotional for Women ($12.95)
1-59337-409-7

A Cup of Comfort for Christians
1-59337-541-7

A Cup of Comfort for Christmas
1-58062-921-0

A Cup of Comfort for Friends
1-58062-622-X

A Cup of Comfort for Grandparents
1-59337-523-9

A Cup of Comfort for Inspiration
1-58062-914-8

A Cup of Comfort for Mothers and Daughters
1-58062-844-3

A Cup of Comfort for Mothers and Sons
1-59337-257-4

A Cup of Comfort for Mothers to Be
1-59337-574-3

A Cup of Comfort for Nurses
1-59337-542-5

A Cup of Comfort for Parents of Children with Autism
1-59337-683-9

A Cup of Comfort for Sisters
1-59337-097-0

A Cup of Comfort for Teachers
1-59337-008-3

A Cup of Comfort for Weddings
1-59337-519-0

A Cup of Comfort for Women
1-58062-748-X

A Cup of Comfort for Women in Love
1-59337-362-7